# JUNGLE LAW

**Mad, Bad, Stupid and Dangerous: True Crime Tales from a Perth Criminal Lawyer**

# HENRY SKLARZ

ISBN: 978-1-922409-47-8
Published by Vivid Publishing
A division of Fontaine Publishing Group
P.O. Box 948, Fremantle
Western Australia 6959
www.vividpublishing.com.au

A catalogue record for this
book is available from the
National Library of Australia

NATIONAL
LIBRARY
OF AUSTRALIA

# Contents

# Acknowledgements

I wish to particularly thank and express gratitude to my son Dan for his valuable assistance in the compilation, creative input and editing of this book. I am most grateful for his insights and valuable contribution.

I also thank Allan Dawson, Rory Feely and Steve Camerlengo for their constructive critiques and contributions during the drafting of this book, to Lucy Ridsdale for final editing and Paul Finn and Geoff Cook for their inspiration to write this book.

I dedicate this book to my wife Jo.

# About the Author

Henry Sklarz was born in Perth in August 1950, the oldest son of Polish immigrants who came to Western Australia after the debacle of World War II. Educated at Trinity College, he attended the University of Western Australia where he graduated with a Bachelor of Arts (double major in psychology), Bachelor of Jurisprudence and Bachelor of Laws. He established his own law firm in the 1980s and has been in legal practice for over 35 years, during which time he worked as a barrister at the Western Australian Independent Bar. While he has worked in various areas of the law, he is a specialist in criminal law acting solely as a defence counsel.

Inspired by decades of working with complex characters in difficult circumstances, and after many dinner-party conversations justifying the work of a defence lawyer, *Jungle Law* is his first book. While he has worked with many case details that are shocking, ugly and tragic, Henry has always kept his sense of humour.

# WARNING

*Jungle Law* contains mature content, drug use, coarse language and depictions of graphic and sexual violence. Reader discretion is advised.

Aboriginal and Torres Strait Islander readers are warned the following contains reference to deceased persons.

In order to protect client confidentiality and maintain anonymity, character names, certain locations, incidents and events may have been changed. I have also used some poetic licence to fictionalise certain details for dramatic effect.

# Preface

At dinner parties when people find out that I am a criminal lawyer, I am often asked, "How can you represent guilty people?" and "How can you sleep at night?" My answer is simply that my clients often have lives as complex as the cases they are embroiled in, and it is not my role or responsibility to enquire into whether they are, in fact, guilty. My professional function requires that upon receiving my instructions and hearing all the relevant information – no matter how gruesome it may be – I advise a client as to whether they have a defence or not. It is the client's decision whether they wish to plead guilty or not guilty. I do not judge them, or their crime, but merely represent their best interest and endeavour to achieve the best result for them within their prevailing circumstances. The criminal judicial system has been established to administer justice, so I am morally resigned to the fact that whatever result I achieve, justice has been served – and so I sleep well at night.

In my first years of practice, building a professional reputation and attracting clients was a challenge. In my first Supreme Court trial in the early 1980s, I represented an alleged rapist who was being tried before a judge and jury. Back then, barristers and judges still wore wigs, gowns and robes in the epochal Supreme Court building. After a gruelling week-long trial, the verdict was read out by the jury foreman acquitting my client of this serious and sinister charge. Having just received my first not guilty verdict, I was positive that such an impressive result would propel me to great heights, as word got out about this momentous achievement. Being a young defence counsel and having notched up this early victory in my professional career I was keen to let the world know how good I was, to foster a good reputation and receive referrals for future work. Surely, a long line of desperate clients would soon come knocking at my office door.

As I left the hallowed halls of the Supreme Court and walked out into the lush gardens, my client, who was grinning from ear to ear, said to me, "Thanks a lot. You were great." I responded, "Well, why don't you tell the world and refer me some work?" When he replied, "I'm sorry mate, but I'm going to keep this whole thing under wraps", I realised that for all my hard work and skill, my reputation would stand mute and the good will generated by the win would go nowhere. Had the effort I put into getting the acquittal materialised as a hit song, I would be receiving royalties and public kudos for many years. Instead, I was simply left with a feeling of bittersweet disappointment.

After remortgaging my house to fund an office lease and furniture, my very first client, Dave, arrived for his initial appointment in my new law practice. Dave's in-struction concerned an assault charge that had something to do with his heavy-handed recovery of a debt. Dave was a young, handsome entrepreneur and I was an ambitious young lawyer. My newly appointed secretary, Mandy, was a beautiful long-legged blonde who had won her heat in the "Miss West Coast" competition at Scarborough Beach the previous weekend. Obviously her bikini body and good looks had aroused the judge's attention sufficiently to allow her to win the day. She had come to work this day – the first day on the job for both of us – wearing loose, white georgette pants with her red knickers underneath clearly visible. Her attire was completely inappropriate for a legal office, however we were all beginners.

Dave was seated opposite me and I was trying very hard to make a good impression as I took notes during the consultation. Without warning or any obvious reason, Mandy pranced into my office and started "filing" the documents of clients I didn't have. Indeed, there was no filing to be done, but my sexy secretary somehow found herself busy in the bottom drawer of the filing cabinet. Dave instinctively turned, saw her red knickers as she bent over the cabinet, looked at me and exclaimed, "How can you work all day with an erection?"

What an awkward start to the week! Mandy turned, blushing, made a quick exit and closed the office door. I looked up at my client and we both burst out laughing. I don't know if Mandy was the victim or the culprit that day, but suffice to say she wore appropriate apparel from then on. She also improved her office demeanour and actually enjoyed a long term of employment with me as my trusty secretary.

After decades of recounting tales of my court cases to amused family and friends, I was convinced to write a book collating the most interesting and bizarre stories of my career as a criminal lawyer. The following chapters are a collection of true short stories of the crimes and punishments of some of my unique clients. Some stories are funny, and others are violent and truly horrifying, however, they are all true. I have changed names in order to protect the identities of all who appear in these pages, so that no one might be tempted to murder me in revenge for revealing their embarrassing and/or treacherous stories. One notable exception is Mr Alvin Kirwan who has given me permission to print his name, as evidenced in the letter reproduced at the end of this book.

In criminal law, as is in most areas of life, fact is often stranger than fiction and in so many cases, "you couldn't make this shit up!"

# Australia's Most Useless Bank Robbers I

Steve was only twenty years of age back in 1990 when he committed the serious offence of armed bank robbery. Over the years leading up to this offence he had lived an aimless life. He was an orphan with no knowledge of who his parents were, and had been cared for by the state, receiving fortnightly welfare payments and little else. He really had drawn the short straw in life. Steve was an unattractive man with a long horse-like face, coarse hair and skin that was blemished with zits and freckles – but his lack of blessings didn't stop there: he was also intellectually challenged. He had stopped living with his foster family when he was only fourteen years of age and had drifted through life from place to place ever since.

On a good day, he would muster the courage to speak to strangers, however, most of the time he kept to himself. His most regular haunt was the doctor's surgery, and he visited it frequently. It didn't matter which doctor he saw, he always spruiked the same set of complaints and problems. They ranged from anxiety to depression, from severe headaches to backaches and so on. This well-rehearsed litany of ailments always got the desired medical result of more painkillers that were, of course, paid for by the state. It would be no surprise to hear that his only escape from this banal and tedious world was through prescription drugs. Left to his own devices, Steve could sit for hours alone in a darkened room, leaning oddly to the left and patiently letting the drugs sugar coat his world. He was not a nuisance to society, and did not have a criminal record of any sort. In the few times that police had cause to speak to him, they had treated him as a harmless vagrant and nothing more. They had far more pressing jobs to attend to.

One day, for some inexplicable reason, he took more prescription tablets than usual and acquired the courage to do something bold and different from his daily drudgery. Robbing a bank seemed like a good idea, as he had little money and decided that the bank could fix that problem. So, he wrote a note that he planned to hand the bank teller, which read, "Give me your fuckin' money cunt. I've got a gun!" He didn't have a gun, but would pretend he did, if necessary. Armed with this note and nothing else – not even a disguise or a frowning face – he went to his local bank soon after it opened for business. There were only a few customers, and he got to a teller without queuing or delay. He handed over the note and stared at the teller as he waited. Quicker than the time it would take to write a withdrawal slip, the teller handed over $601 cash. Steve grabbed the cash and promptly left the bank on foot, leaving his note as a souvenir.

He didn't know how much he had collected but it looked and felt like a lot more cash than he had ever held before. Some fifty meters down the road he went into a clothing shop – not to hide, but to buy clothes that he was in dire need of. He spent over forty minutes there trying on different clothes and eventually bought a jumper, some t-shirts and two pairs of trousers. As he was paying for the clothes with the stolen cash, the medication wore off and Steve became overwhelmed with remorse and shame for what he had just done. With the shopping bag of clothes and the rest of the cash in hand, he returned to the bank to surrender himself. However, as he approached the bank, he found that the doors were firmly shut and the bank had been closed for business due to the robbery.

Steve stood in front of the locked doors thumping loudly on them with his fist. He could see into the bank and even see the people inside, but no one was opening the door. He kept knocking persistently. After a while, the teller recognised him and got the bank manager who cautiously opened the front door. Steve said forthrightly,

"I was here before and I feel bad and want to give myself up." As he said this, the door was fully opened for him and he handed the manager the shopping bag of new clothes and the balance of the cash, which now totalled $224. Steve then spent some time chatting to the manager while waiting for the police to arrive. This would have been an interesting conversation to overhear.

Steve was charged with armed robbery because he pretended to be armed with a gun. For this charge, the law considers that even the pretence of having a gun fits within the definition of the charge because the perpetrator is using it for the same effect: to intimidate and cause terror in order to rob. Due to the seriousness of the charge, Steve was denied bail and was remanded in custody for four months before the matter progressed to the Supreme Court of Western Australia where he pleaded guilty. As his counsel at sentencing, I referred to Steve's robbery as a bizarre event and suggested that in the circumstances, the bank staff had suffered minimal trauma. Further, the robbery had been quick and only targeted one teller. I contrasted his robbery against the classic balaclava-and-shotgun bank robbery somewhat reminiscent of a Tarantino film. I continued that the inconvenience to the bank had been partly rectified by Steve's prompt return and the subsequent recovery of the clothes and cash. In fact, Steve's actions had been so ludicrous and inane that even the bank staff would have likely found some humour in his reappearance. I also emphasised to the Court that it was most unlikely that Steve would reoffend as he had now beaten his addiction to prescription drugs and had learnt his lesson, having spent the last four months in custody.

The prosecutor agreed with my sentencing submissions and told the Court that this was one of those rare cases of armed robbery where imprisonment was not warranted. He said that an appropriate disposition would be probation and a community service order. Fortunately for Steve, the judge agreed and placed him on probation, which allowed Steve to walk out of the Court with me instead of returning to prison to serve between four and ten years.

Some days later, after some newspaper and media publicity of this rare bank robbery, I received a thank-you letter from Steve, which he signed, "bank bandit." I wondered what lesson he had in fact learnt. As I said, he wasn't exactly the sharpest tool in the shed or the brightest bulb in the chandelier.

# Tattoos, Devils and Arseholes

B rody was a young and well-recognised tattooist. He had been gifted with the hands of an artisan and had the artistry of a portrait painter. His tattoos were primarily his own creations, but he also reproduced classic and popular images upon request. Not only was he talented, he was also ambitious. His goal was to have a blossoming career and recognition Australia-wide, even though his current tattoo parlour was a humble two-room studio in Belmont, a working-class suburb near the luxurious Crown Casino in Perth.

Covered in tattoos himself, he was a living, breathing advertisement for his artistic services and it was no surprise that within the industry he was nicknamed "Magic Fingers". Upon the blank canvas of a patch of skin, he would conjure provocative and meaningful art, though admittedly, the art meant more to the wearer than to any curious observer. The decision to get a tattoo is often impulsive, made on the spur of the moment, though it has the obvious consequences of permanency. It is important to get a tattoo that has perpetual relevance, particularly so because in old age the skin sags and the wrinkled image can blur into an embarrassing mess. When Brody completed a tattoo it stood out proud on young, taut skin. Obviously, one might question just how provoking and meaningful it would still be with the passage of time, but that is not ours to judge.

Unfortunately for Brody, the events of one busy evening threatened his tattooing career and aspirations. A young female customer accused him of sexually assaulting her, alleging that he digitally penetrated her vagina while she was being tattooed. This incident had come about when the attractive female, in her mid-twenties, came into his parlour and asked about getting a tattoo. She was alone, and dressed in an alluring top and fashionably ripped brief shorts. He was also alone, having just finished with his previous customer before she walked in. She told him she wanted a small black devil tattooed on her left buttock. This was her first tattoo and she thought it would be best to start with the devil. He showed her his portfolio of demonic creatures and she chose a cute devil with horns and a tail without much fuss, but asked that it be a little smaller – no more than three centimetres in size – and some five centimetres from her bum crack.

Brody quoted a price that was agreeable to her and

then asked her to remove her shorts and panties, so they wouldn't get ink on them or get in the way, and so he could have ready access to the buttock to apply the tattoo. She obliged him and lay face down on the cushioned plastic table he used for his clients. She waited for Magic Fingers to create his masterpiece on her left buttock, which was now shining under the bright parlour lights, and casually propped herself up on her elbows and started texting on her mobile phone. Brody was at the other end stretching her buttock skin taut and sketching the image. It transpires that while Brody's magic fingers were at work, her fingers were also busy texting her boyfriend and updating him on her devilish new hallmark.

When Brody finished the tattoo, she checked it out in the mirror with much pleasure, got dressed and paid him, without making any comment about his magic fingers. Later it transpired that she had been texting her boyfriend saying that she had been violated by Brody who, she said, was sticking his fingers into her vagina while tattooing her in the nude. She later told her boyfriend that in any event, she was happy with the little devil and did not intend to make any formal complaint. It was only at her boyfriend's insistence that she subsequently made a complaint to police, which culminated in the charge. It was alleged that Brody had penetrated her vagina with his fingers without consent whilst tattooing the devil. Brody was devastated with this allegation, and if it wasn't so serious, one might have quipped that it was the devil's work that got him into trouble.

Brody pleaded not guilty to the charge and the matter went to trial before a judge and jury. The prosecution alleged that Brody had deliberately and without consent placed his fingers into the young woman's vagina while creating the tattoo. The prosecution also alleged that she had made a timely complaint of the offence to her boyfriend by text. The boyfriend, therefore, was to be called as a witness and I, as defence counsel, had the challenging task of cross-examining him, as well as the female complainant.

It was in the prosecution's interest to call the boyfriend to give evidence of the complaint, to lend weight to the allegation that the incident had indeed occurred and hadn't been concocted. However, during my cross-examination of him, it became painfully obvious that it had been him, not the purported victim, who had initiated the complaint to the police. He was relying on his girlfriend's comments and accusations, which under cross-examination seemed fanciful. Overall, the boyfriend sounded most unconvincing. Also, it wasn't hard to undermine her credibility and cast aspersions on the veracity of this bogus complaint. As my client sat nervously in the accused's dock, it was up to me to work some magic in front of the jury and persuade them that there was reasonable doubt the incident occurred at all.

Brody elected to give evidence, even though like all people accused of a crime, he had no obligation to do so. Each accused is presumed innocent at their trial. The prosecution has the onus of proving the charge to the necessary standard of proof – that is, being proven beyond reasonable doubt. In other words, because it is the prosecution who brings the charge against the accused, it is the prosecution who has the sole burden of proof and the accused can choose to do nothing and say nothing. The accused has no burden to prove their innocence.

Brody took the stand and recited the oath to tell the truth, the whole truth and nothing but the truth. He told the jury how he drew and tattooed the black devil onto his client's buttock, as instructed. He further told the jury how he had stretched the skin to make her buttock taut as was necessary so he could apply the ink. He said that while he had been obliged to work intimately and necessarily close to her anus and vagina, he had not penetrated either orifice, nor had he had any need or desire to do so while applying the tattoo. Brody concluded his evidence by telling the jury that when he finished the devil tattoo, his customer – the complainant – while still naked from the waist down, admired the devil in the mirror before she put her clothes on. She told him she was thrilled with his workmanship and happily paid him without any mention of inappropriate behaviour. In fact, she had taken his business card as she left the parlour, saying she would refer her friends to him.

After hearing all the evidence, the jury took a short time to deliberate and reached a unanimous verdict of not guilty, thereby acquitting my client of that sinister charge.

His name and reputation clear, Brody moved interstate to continue his career as a tattoo artist, however, he endeavoured to avoid, where possible, devils and arseholes.

Facial tattoos obviously mean different things to different people – especially when they are part of someone's cultural tradition. However, it is difficult to imagine a more stupid depiction than the tattoo on the left cheek of the face of a young male hooligan who opted for the words "FUCK THE POLICE". This statement was emblazoned in bold black lettering and was about four centimetres square. Therefore it was not surprising that one evening, while travelling on the train, he got into a fight with two passengers, who happened to be off-duty policemen accompanied by their girlfriends. They took exception to the tattoo and its message and approached him in disgust, asking for an explanation as they said that they were police. The hooligan exploded in rage, and started head butting and punching them. The fight went on for a short time and both off-duty officers were injured. As it turned out, although the train carriage was fitted with CCTV equipment, it didn't capture the incident as it occurred directly underneath the camera itself and so was out of view. After my client was charged with assaulting the officers the matter proceeded to a trial. For the prosecution to succeed with a conviction they had to prove that my client was actually involved, so identifying him was crucial.

Prior to trial, the investigating officer prepared a photo

board identity sheet for the train witnesses and the two girlfriends to see if they could recognise and identify the accused. Such a photo board is an A4 sheet comprising a sequence of 12 mug shots of different criminals, including the accused, all of whom are similar looking. The photos are numbered and these numbers refer to the details of that individual. The photos are the same size and generally in black and white.

In this case, because the accused had the "FUCK THE POLICE" tattoo on his left cheek, the police had superimposed the same words on the left cheeks of the men in the other 11 mug shots. This was supposed to make it fair for the accused – otherwise he would have been readily identified by the witnesses. It is no wonder that at the trial he had two Band-Aid strips covering the tattoo, trying to hide it from the jury. However, the Band-Aids were as obvious as the tattoo itself.

Unfortunately for my client, he was positively identified at trial and subsequently convicted. So on this occasion, and despite his tattoo, it was he who was "fucked" by the police.

# Cocaine Cowboy

During the late 1980s, Dylan worked by day as a garbage collector for one of the shires in Perth and by night he dealt drugs in the nightclubs whose rubbish bins he had collected earlier. Dylan was twenty-two years old, a tall, handsome lad, who could have easily been a male model. He had left school when he was only fourteen because he was a poor student and hadn't had a caring mentor or a responsible parent to encourage him to continue. His poor education soon evolved into an urban wisdom of survival as he entered the workplace at the lowest level of an unskilled labourer. He had to fend for himself and became streetwise very quickly. Doing various labouring jobs gave him an awareness and appreciation of his own impressive physique. He got interested in body-building, and to complement his gym workouts he undertook the servile job of collecting rubbish bins to maintain his fitness, as it required him to lift heavy bins and run between loads of rubbish.

Over the next few years Dylan's disciplined routine of gym and work gave him an even better physique and a renewed persona with newborn confidence. He loved the nightlife and became very much a lady's man. His popularity escalated amongst the ladies particularly those who didn't know that he worked as a garbage collector during the day. For those ladies it was sufficient for them to look at him simply as an Adonis and admire him accordingly.

Dylan was burning the candle at each end. He would start his gruelling work shift early in the morning and then rave at the nightclubs late each night. After many months of work and fun he started to burn out and stopped going to the gym. A concerned friend saw this lull and suggested to him that he take cocaine to lift his spirits and energy. Dylan embraced that idea and it wasn't long before the trilogy of drugs, work and fun ruled his world. His drug habit intensified and started to become expensive; it cost him a lot more than he could afford as a garbo. He had to earn more money and the simple solution was to deal drugs.

He started selling cocaine at first, simply to make enough cash to buy a sufficient amount for his daily needs. As his sales soared and his clientele flourished, he started to make thousands of dollars a night dealing at the various nightclubs that he frequented. A typical night would reap him over $3,000 cash. He was earning so much that it made little sense to keep his servile job, however, he did continue it as a ruse to conceal his real job, which was now dealing in cocaine.

Being young and somewhat naïve, he threw his money around and became very popular with those wanting drugs and fun. Like most drug dealers, his ego got in the way of better judgment. His hubris ascended into its own orbit. Girls he met at the nightclubs were swept off their feet with his generosity and flamboyance. On one occasion he was keen on a working-class girl he'd met on a Friday night whilst dealing and partying. He was smitten with her beauty and made her an irresistible proposition. He asked her to get her passport and meet him at the Perth International Airport at midnight that night so they could fly first class to Paris for an extended weekend. For her, this was "love at first flight". Her only worry was what excuse she would give her boss for not being at work on Monday. That minor dilemma was subsequently resolved by calling her boss from the Ritz Carlton in Paris and telling him that she was unwell and unable to come to work that day. I am sure she still talks about that trip of a lifetime.

With all the trappings of a successful drug dealer, he couldn't help himself but buy a red 328GTS Ferrari – the same model that Magnum PI drove on the TV series. Of course, the only way he could finance this Ferrari was with undeclared cash, and this was the very moment he came to the attention of the police. The Ferrari-driving, globetrotting garbage collector had his days numbered. This highflyer was soon to come crashing down to earth.

When Dylan was arrested the police confiscated the Ferrari and found half a million dollars in cash buried in the backyard of his rental home. He fully cooperated with the police investigation and after pleading guilty to serious drug dealing; he received a long term of eight years imprisonment commensurate with his audacity and profile.

During the time I was taking his instructions, I asked Dylan why he dealt in drugs. His response was rather obvious, in that he said that the temptations and rewards were so great he couldn't resist, and there was no future in being a garbo anyway. Unfortunately for this garbo, though, his work in jail would turn out to be similarly "on the nose".

The face of drugs is usually a youthful one – that of a dealer who is charismatic and enterprising – and this young entrepreneur of immorality will sell or supply drugs to the needy addict and the fun-loving partygoer, alike. The history of illicit drugs has evolved from leaf cannabis to hydroponic cannabis, and up to hard drugs such as cocaine, heroin, ecstasy, MDMA and methamphetamine, any one of which is likely to lead to addiction with its associated mental and physical health problems.

The illicit drug trade is a multi-billion-dollar international market that is exponentially growing. At present, methamphetamine is most popular due to its relative ease of manufacture and affordability. Its most common street name is "ice" and it is highly addictive; a user can be hooked on the drug from the first time they use it. It is associated with serious health conditions, including memory loss, psychotic behaviour and aggression. The deadly combination of psychosis and aggression can lead users to commit acts of horrendous violence such as assaults and even murder. Sadly, it is the case nowadays that drugs of this nature underscore the majority of violent crimes that are committed on a daily basis, and that clog our health system with aggressive and unpredictable addicts.

On a mid-morning break during a drug trial, I was chatting with a senior detective from the Organised Crime Squad who was a prosecution witness. To pass the time I asked him whether he was involved in any other interesting investigations. He went on to tell me that a large-scale ecstasy laboratory was being set up on the southern outskirts of Perth. Police intelligence was that a crime syndicate was preparing for a drug cook-up, which would be done by a rogue chemist flown in from Queensland for that purpose. Unfortunately for the crime syndicate, though, the chemist was arrested in Darwin and could not complete his flight to Perth. The syndicate had everything ready in the lab kitchen except the chef. At this point of frustration, an apprentice motor mechanic, who was also a bikie associate, put his hand up and volunteered to do the cook-up even though he had an IQ nudging the lowest quartile. He consulted Google and started the cook-up with the various dangerous substances and volatile gases they emitted, which he had never dealt with or even heard of before.

Subsequently, the Police raided the drug lab and it took them the better part of a day to safely remove the apparatus and clean up the chemicals. In the mess, the police found two thousand freshly pressed tablets ready for sale to Perth's party scene. Each tablet was embossed with a star, obviously to make it look alluring. Fortunately these tablets did not make it into the community, as scientific tests revealed that each tablet was lethal. Hundreds of lives of unsuspecting users were spared the likelihood of a painful death.

# The Granny Killer

In this age of equality, it is appropriate that I give credence to stories in which women take their place in the law and under the law. I have generally found the female gender to be less predatory than their male counterparts, but they can still be as deadly.

Recently, one early morning while I was having breakfast, I received a telephone call from a woman requesting that I represent her fifty-seven-year-old mother, Kristina, who had been charged with murdering her own seventy-six-year-old mother. Kristina was in fact the official carer of her aged mother, and her daughter was an eloquent young lady studying psychology at the University of Western Australia. She was living at home with her mother and now-deceased grandmother. The daughter had a boyfriend and was looking forward to moving out of the family home and settling down with him.

Her mother and grandmother had fostered a love–hate relationship: at times they got on well and at other times they were less harmonious. In evidence later given before the Supreme Court, a neighbour said that he heard yelling and threats from the household, some six months before the macabre incident occurred. Kristina was screaming, "I can't stand the fucking bitch, I want to kill her." It was obvious that the domestic environment was in serious disharmony.

Kristina was a germaphobe and had an obsessive personality. She would bleach the floors every day and clean the house to a meticulous standard. Mind you, the cleaning wasn't a bad idea as she had four dogs living in the rental house. The resident canines ranged in size from large to small, being a great Dane, a Staffordshire terrier, a shih tzu and a Chihuahua, and they had the run of the small government estate house, which stood on a block no bigger than 200 square meters. All four dogs slept on special bedding in Kristina's bedroom and were let out the back to do their business. Occasionally, Kristina's daughter took the dogs for walks; she was the only person fit enough to do so. The smell of bleach and other cleaning products permeated the entire home, which housed all seven of them – the three humans and four dogs.

Her mother and grandmother would fight bitterly over absurd domestic matters such as cleaning, washing and so on. It appeared to be an ambivalent relationship where at times they needed each other and were pleasant, and at other times they couldn't stand each other, and expressed their animosity with verbal abuse and insults. There was always some issue or problem that provoked the acrimony between them, yet they would bury the hatchet around six o'clock each night and sit down together to watch the Channel 7 news. They both seemed to find it soothing to watch and hear about other people's misfortunes on the news: it eased the burden of their own miserable lives. Kristina's husband was long gone and lived in the eastern states. Her adult son was always looking for an excuse to stay away from the feuding family, and wasn't around either.

Because of the discord, the grandmother started to look for alternative accommodation despite her frail health and old age. She couldn't walk far without a walking stick so exercising the dogs was impossible, however getting away from the home became a priority. At her late stage in life she should have enjoyed the solace of Kristina's companionship and care, however the opposite was true. She must have felt that she needed to escape from her daughter and find a more comfortable and safe refuge.

A weekly visit from the Jehovah's Witness ameliorated the grandmother's anguish. Two caring JW devotees would come to the front door and speak privately to the grandmother. These visits infuriated Kristina and more often than not they caused an escalation of the friction between her and her mother. The arguments would become heated and quickly reach boiling point. On one such occasion, late in the afternoon, the daughter returned home after walking the Staffy and shih tzu to find that her grandmother wasn't home. She asked her mother about the unexpected absence and was told that while she wasn't sure, she thought the grandmother had left with the Jehovah's Witnesses.

This explanation must have been plausible to the daughter, as she raised no concerns during the weeks that went by without any word from her grandmother. The household even enjoyed some relative normality, until one evening the daughter let the dogs out into the backyard for a short romp and to do their business. The backyard was totally fenced off, with the only access being through the back door of the house and the side front gate. When the daughter called the dogs to come back inside, the great Dane did not return. She went out, and found him in the small, enclosed backyard, which was sandy and stark. The dogs also had access to the side yard, which continued around the house to where the rubbish bins were kept near the side front gate. This gate would only be used on rubbish collection days when the bins were taken out. Otherwise, it was a secluded area of the yard that was mainly used by the dogs.

When the daughter came around into the side yard to see what the dog was up to, she saw the great Dane biting and scratching at something on the ground near the bins. As she came closer, she saw some corrugated tin sheets lying on the ground, partly obscuring something that she couldn't quite make out. The ground beneath the tin sheets was not flat but something of a mound and the dog was busy at its task, chewing, what she realised with horror, was a human skull. She screamed and recoiled, startling the dog, who retreated, stumbling over some empty bleach bottles as it backed away from the grave.

Kristina was not home when this happened, and the daughter urgently telephoned the police, telling them about the dog's gruesome discovery of human remains in what appeared to be a shallow grave. The police promptly arrived and sealed off the entire area, including the house and all its contents, as part of a crime scene. The police forensic team arrived at the same moment as a taxi from which Kristina alighted with bags of shopping. When told of what had been found, Kristina appeared to be shocked and horrified and was consoled by her daughter and a female police officer. At the time, no one mentioned the missing grandmother, but it wasn't long before the police identified the skull and bones as belonging to her. After a short police investigation, Kristina was charged with the murder of her mother.

When I spoke to Kristina at Melaleuca Women's Prison and Remand Integration Centre, she told me that she hadn't killed her mother and explained that her mother had left with the ladies from the Jehovah's Witness and must have been murdered by them and later brought back to the premises and left in the shallow grave. She tried to explain that access could have easily been gained through the side gate, near the rubbish bins where her mother was put to rest. As much as I dislike being disturbed on weekends by Jehovah's Witnesses and their intrusive door knocking, I found it difficult to believe such morally upright people might kill an old lady and generally behave in such an evil and despicable way. But as her defence counsel, I did not judge my client, as my duty was to represent her, pursuant to her instructions. The defence she gave that day was therefore put before the jury at trial.

As I have already explained, every accused is innocent of any criminal charge unless and until it is proved beyond reasonable doubt that they are guilty. On a charge as serious as murder, for which life imprisonment applies, an accused is highly motivated to challenge the allegations and give themselves every chance of beating the wrap, rather than plead guilty outright. Besides, having a trial in the Supreme Court is a memorable experience, so memorable, in fact, that you could get a lifetime to reflect on it.

The prosecution alleged that my client had killed her mother in the house by inflicting fatal stab injuries, then dragged her outside and buried her by the bins. They asserted that she then used bottles of liquid bleach to accelerate the decomposition of the body and mask the scent of rotting flesh. Bleach contains chemicals such as sodium hypochlorite and chlorine, which kill mould and remove grime and stains when used in a domestic setting, however, when used in large quantities, bleach does more than kill germs, it disintegrates flesh and organs.

Because the house had been kept so obsessively clean

and sterile, there was very little forensic evidence in the residence except for some traces of blood on the back doorstep. There was evidence on the leg bones of the deceased, however, indicating that a sharp weapon had inflicted multiple serious wounds. The state's case was circumstantial, relying partly on the acrimonious relationship between the two women and partly on the neighbour overhearing the death threats, which indicated a motive for the murder. Adding to suspicion, Kristina had withdrawn money from her mother's bank account after her disappearance and also a knife and a pair of scissors had been found in the shallow grave.

It was submitted by the prosecutor to the jury that my client had snapped and stabbed her mother to death and then dragged the body around the side of the house and buried it, hoping it would totally disintegrate with the excessive liquid bleach she poured over it. The post-mortem examination referred to injuries on the head and multiple stab wounds to the deceased's legs. The attack must have been ferocious and persistent.

The defence case that I brought in part challenged the proposition that the accused could have dragged the dead body due to a severe, and indeed incapacitating, back injury. Further, it was put to the jury that the corpse could not have been in situ for the whole time the woman had been missing, as the dogs would have detected it earlier – probably immediately after the alleged murder and not weeks later. In an attempt to prove this point, a veterinary expert was called, who gave evidence that a dog has an estimated three hundred million odorant receptors compared to the five million or so that a human has. In other words, a dog's smelling capacity is sixty times stronger than our own; a dog can smell objects buried up to ten metres underground. This defence submission was presented to show that because the dogs did not detect the corpse until weeks after the alleged murder, it went to prove that the corpse had not been in situ the whole time, and must have been put there weeks later – just before it was discovered. This proposition gave credence to the supposition that the Jehovah's Witnesses had something to do with the grandmother's disappearance, demise and reappearance.

The theatre of the courtroom can be fascinating when the defence counsel raises novel and interesting propositions in an attempt to conjure up "reasonable doubt" in the jury's mind. However, it is the jurors who finally decide the guilt or innocence of the accused. They comprise a cross-section of individuals from society who bring their collective worldly experiences and common sense to deliberations. In Kristina's case, the jury deliberated for three hours and unanimously convicted her of the murder of her mother. Hopefully, both mother and daughter are now at peace with each other – one rests in prison, while the other rests in peace.

# The Prostitutes

I t is said that "clothes maketh the man" and traditionally
– though perhaps to a lesser extent now – people's attire
tends to match their profession. For example, bankers,
lawyers and funeral directors wear suits; chefs, flight at-
tendants and police officers wear uniforms; construction
workers and tradies on site wear hi-vis vests, and so on.
There is a lot that can be inferred about a person from
the clothes they wear. To a large extent, their "uniform"
projects their socio-economic status in society, and while
one shouldn't judge a book by it's cover, it is nevertheless a
fair indicator of the person.

In 1980, I had the pleasure of representing Sandy and
Cindy, two prostitutes charged with a minor matter of
disorderly behaviour. On the morning in question, they
had finished a hard night's work in the brothel where they
worked and were walking home at around 6:30am. In a
manner well suited to their profession, they were cheer-
ful and cheeky when they came across a couple having

an early al fresco breakfast at a roadside cafe. The couple, a jowly, red-faced husband and his dowdy wife, were both retired primary school teachers who had taught Grade Three children (he, mathematics, and she, religious studies) throughout their entire careers. Neither had a sense of humour. Maybe that came from dealing with ratty children all day long. The offence against Sandy and Cindy was that after receiving a judgmental look from the old couple, they had showed off their youthful breasts and said, "Would you like some milk with your cornflakes?"

Sandy and Cindy were obviously used to showing off their breasts to customers (and others!) however, this couple took exception and reported them to the police. The police had no trouble finding Sandy and Cindy as they were very recognisable with their green and orange hair adorned with Indian feathers, ultra-short miniskirts and towering high heels. At the time of apprehension, they were walking hand-in-hand, carefree and sassy.

As a result of the incident and the subsequent charges, they made an appointment to see me to obtain legal advice and representation. They came to my office together at 11am, after a full night's work. I remember the moment clearly, as it was in the middle of my working morning. Oddly enough, they were still dressed in the same attire as they had been when described by the couple at the time of the offence. Obviously, these clothes were their "work uniforms", and one could easily judge this book by its cover – *prostitutes*.

I was thirty at this time, and had been practising law for a few years, but had never seen such a sight as these girls in my office before. The environment of the office was usually business-like and reserved. And not only did they completely look the part, they also swore like troopers: everything that came from their mouths was "fuck this" and "fuck that..." For my part, I was studiously taking notes when all of a sudden, one of the girls spread her legs right in front of me and said, "This is our money box". I looked at her naked crutch and couldn't believe that this was happening in my office. With her legs still unashamedly open, she grinned and continued, "And this money box can pay your fee." Clearing my throat, I replied, "I was hoping for money, as I have an expensive wife." There was much laughter and her legs, like the conversation, came to a close.

When the matter finally came before the Court, Sandy and Cindy looked magnificent in their work uniforms. Their appearance was a breath of fresh air in the stuffy courtroom. They admitted the offence without shame and apologised for any discourtesy their comments had caused the two prudes. The magistrate, unlike the complaining retirees, had the common sense to see the triviality of the incident and dismissed the matter without conviction or penalty. Sandy and Cindy were very pleased with the outcome and wanted to pay me in kind. I was flattered by their proposition but again pointed out that I was married and it was only 10:30am. I suggested that it would be best if they would be so kind as to pay their bill in cash.

Some years later, I had the challenge of representing Ms Lee who was a pretty prostitute, originally from Singapore. She was only twenty-one years old and had a petite, sexy figure with light-coloured silky skin and long black hair. She was always well groomed and presentable, however her loud red lipstick and skimpy clothes sometimes gave her away. She said she was studying microbiology at the University of Western Australia, though if her job was anything to go by, she also had a strong interest in human biology.

Ms Lee's charm permeated her character with desirability. Most of her clients were middle-aged wealthy Asian men who were most generous to her. Particularly when she told them her sad story of being alone in Western Australia and having to earn money prostituting herself so she could send money to her sick mother in Singapore.

She was so good at her job that it wasn't long before a client became besotted with her and bought her clothes, flowers and gifts. This lovesick client heard Ms Lee's lament of how her sick mother needed urgent heart surgery and how she couldn't afford it. These tales of woe opened her client's heart, who in turn opened his wallet to her. He was most concerned about her mother's welfare and was convinced that she should have her expensive heart surgery. In the fray, he also proposed to Ms Lee, and requested that they marry soon so that he, as husband and son-in-law, could provide for her and her sickly mother.

After knowing her for only a short period of time, he gave her $2,000 cash and then a few months later, another $9,700 – supposedly for the mother's outstanding medical fees. Several months down the track, Ms Lee telephoned him from Singapore and claimed that her mother was unfortunately in a coma and required urgent intensive nursing. She persuaded him to send a further $3,500. Love-struck and genuinely concerned for his future bride and mother-in-law, he spontaneously flew to Singapore to surprise his bride and give his support, and to personally attend to their welfare. However, upon arriving in Singapore, he was told by Ms Lee that her mother was too weak to see him. After a short visit, he returned home without having seen the mother, but not before he paid a further $3,000 for her medical expenses.

Upon her subsequent return to Perth, Ms Lee cunningly milked him of $4,500 to supposedly pay for her own international student fees, $3,000 for her mother's further medical treatment, $5,000 for university enrolment and another $3,000 for her mother's pacemaker which had to be installed to save the phantom woman from dying. It wasn't long before his presents and cash gifts totalled more than $30,000 that he paid out of his hard-earned savings.

As he tried to get closer to Ms Lee, she started avoiding him – apparently because he had served his purpose. She told him she had to leave him and return to Singapore to be by her mother's side. The heart-broken benefactor accepted Ms Lee's departure as unavoidable, but hoped it was temporary. Later, he received a letter from Ms Lee, supposedly sent from Singapore. Her deception included redirecting letters to him via Singapore to fool him into thinking that she was in that country caring for her mother rather than still working as a prostitute in Perth, which was the reality.

In her letters, Ms Lee told him that her mother's surgery had gone well and that her mother was leaving hospital under her care. In the last letter, she added that she had met a fellow in Singapore who had proposed to her and she had agreed to marry him. She concluded with the touching words, "don't be angry or upset, we can still be friends. I will always keep our friendship in my heart." There was no mention of his heart-felt generosity or the large amount of cash he had obliged her. The tenor of the letter was more terminal than her mother's illness.

Within days of this letter, however, the charade unravelled dramatically when he spotted her by chance in a Perth restaurant dining with another infatuated client. This was at a time when she was supposed to be in Singapore looking after her sickly mother. The obvious truth of the matter dawned on him and despite his shattered emotions, he went straight to the police. He complained that he would not have given Ms Lee all that money if he had known that her lament was false. He had been lied to and felt cheated by Ms Lee, whom he loved and trusted.

The police penned a detailed statement from the duped lover and charged her with obtaining $33,700 cash by false pretences. I represented Ms Lee when she went on trial at the District Court, having pleaded not guilty. She was confident that she could persuade the jury with her charm to believe her story that she wasn't a scamming prostitute but always intended to repay these moneys, which had been loans and were not fraudulent benefits. She said in her evidence that the stories she told her client about her mother were partly true. She in fact did have a mother. The jury, having heard his and her sides of the sordid one-way love story, convicted her. The prostitute who duped her lovesick client was sentenced to three years jail for her crimes and cynical abuse of the relationship.

Her punishment might seem harsh, however it was meant to serve as a sentence of general deterrence to the community and a warning that the courts consider fraudulent acquisition of money more serious than outright stealing. It is difficult to believe that in these modern times of sugardaddy.com, Instagram princesses and online dating, that this scenario would be an isolated case. Deception and fraud through the use of sex are commonplace in our society.

As we all know, sex sells. Media commercials with their sexy babe or hunky Adonis sell everything and anything, from toothpaste to haemorrhoid cream and face wipes to arse wipes.

On another occasion, I represented a prostitute who was charged with possessing cannabis. I took particular care in explaining to her that she should wear something feminine and appropriate when she was due to appear in court. This would make a good impression on the magistrate and could help soften the police accusations so that I could get a good result for her, such as a minor fine.

The day of the court appearance arrived and so did she, wearing a light chiffon dress that was totally see-through. It was completely inappropriate for a court of law, but it was her expression of femininity and her large fake breasts stood out like melons with cherries on top. Little was left to the imagination, and she certainly had the attention of all those present in court who, for a moment, probably forgot their own tribulations. Her case was being called next and I had no time to cover my client up with anything except my suit coat. This at least would cover her breasts and hopefully the waist-high bar table would hide the rest of her, including her visible crotch.

The case was called by the court orderly and I approached the bar table with my client wearing my coat. The female magistrate glared at me, no doubt wondering why I was not appropriately dressed in a proper suit, and was instead wearing a shirt and tie but no coat. Before the magistrate could reproach me, "Your Worship," I said, (as they were called then), "I had to lend my coat to my client for the obvious reason." The magistrate said, "And what reason is that?" and I retorted, "In fact, there are two reasons and they are now both covered."

# The Deadly Doctor

John was a young and handsome doctor just four years out of medical school. He dedicated himself to his work and swore the Hippocratic Oath to uphold ethical and scientific standards in his professional practice of medicine. This oath has its origin in the Greek physician Hippocrates, and is a promise made by medical practitioners to maintain professional standards and be accountable for their actions. It is a promise that obliges doctors to conduct themselves in a proper and ethical manner and to save lives. This was the pledge made by John.

John's workload was onerous and involved long hours and demanding patients. His life was further complicated by the fact that he was living in a small coastal country town in Western Australia's beautiful but isolated south-west, away from family and friends. However, having realised his ambition to be a doctor, he was prepared to embrace these challenges in the pursuit of his medical career. During the summer he would enjoy a swim at the picturesque local beach, which was always a welcoming respite from the burden of hospital duties. The golden sands of the beach crowned the turquoise waters of a lovely inlet and it was a popular destination for locals and tourists alike, due to its unique beauty and closeness to the town. There was no better place to soak in the soothing ocean and lay on the sun-blessed sands. Serenity and beauty captivated all the senses.

One early morning at the end of a night shift he got the chance to have a break and took the opportunity to drive to that beach for a swim in the pristine waters of the Indian Ocean. John was driving his Hilux utility, a four-wheel drive crew-cab vehicle with a roo bar in front of its long white bonnet. Roo bars are a common accessory on vehicles used in the Australian countryside. They are used to protect motorists, and their engines, in the event of a collision with an unpredictable kangaroo. The long, gently winding road to the beach had a bitumen surface with no markings, and was bordered by gravel shoulders. He was driving at the speed limit of 90km/h as there was no hurry, and he had the road to himself. It wasn't long, however, before a cloud of fatigue descended upon him and he drifted off and crossed over onto the opposite side of the road.

That same morning a beautiful seventeen-year-old student had been at that beach for an early morning swim before school. She was still a probationary driver, having obtained her driver's licence only nine months before. She was alone and was driving her mother's Mitsubishi Magna sedan back to town on the same road. She was driving in an orderly manner, however as fate would have it, she approached John's oncoming ute. Thinking on her feet, she reasoned that the ute, which was drifting into her lane, would continue its trajectory, so she tried to evade the danger by deliberately steering across to the side of the road where the ute should have been travelling. In other words, she crossed over to the wrong side of the road to avoid the imminent collision. She had very little time to react and made the manoeuvre instinctively.

Tragically, at that very moment, the young doctor roused himself and corrected his steering back to his side of the road. The head on collision was violent. Each vehicle was travelling at approximately 90km/hr. The Magna concertinaed like the closing bellows of an accordion and the young woman suffered massive injuries even though she was wearing her seatbelt. The doctor's ute, due to its larger mass, received minor damage to its rigid roo bar and its driver only received a dislocated shoulder injury.

After the disastrous moment of collision, time seemed to slow down and John removed himself from his ute and went anxiously to the aid of the young victim. With some difficulty, he was able to extract her from the wreckage and comfort her in his lap beside her crushed car. He held her in his arms consoling her and talking to her as she expired.

The bitter irony of the accident could have inspired a Shakespearean drama, from the tragedy of the girl dying in the arms of the person who caused her death, to the disbelief of a doctor who by his actions had terminated life instead of saving it. During the subsequent trial proceedings the Court rejected the defence of accident and convicted John of dangerous driving causing death. His momentary lapse of attention put his medical career at risk and would likely carry a sentence of imprisonment. Sentencing was adjourned to the following day to allow the prosecutor, and myself as his defence counsel, to present sentencing submissions. Obviously, my paramount consideration was to rescue my client's future and his professional career from the very real threat of immediate imprisonment.

Regrettably, the legal precedents as outlined by the criminal Court of Appeal, and upon which the prosecutor relied, pointed towards the likelihood of immediate imprisonment for a term of four to eight years. On the sentencing day my client was contrite and had prepared himself for the worst. Imprisonment was likely despite the fact that he was extremely remorseful, had no prior convictions, and that such a sanction would devastate his medical career.

The courts regard imprisonment as a sanction of last

resort. Every other punishment is considered before the Court relents to impose custody. Consideration is given to matters of personal and general deterrence. In this case, there was no need for personal deterrence as the young doctor had learnt his lesson and was unlikely to reoffend. However, general deterrence was still an important factor, communicating to other drivers that they are likely to be seriously punished for driving dangerously – which not only includes breaking the speed limit but also inattention. As the Court reconvened, Her Honour opened the sentencing proceedings by announcing that she had received a letter from the mother of the deceased girl and intended to read the contents in open Court and incorporate it into the transcript.

My first reaction to the presence of the letter was one of pessimism. I expected it to be the mother's mournful petition declaring how my client's criminal negligence had devastated her and her family and that in retribution, a considerable term of imprisonment should be imposed. However, I was very wrong in this assessment of the grieving mother, who had stoically sat through the entire trial. In her letter the mother asked the Court not to imprison the young doctor because it would ruin his life and his medical career. Her precious daughter's life was ruined and that was enough, she wrote. There was no need to ruin another life, especially the life of a young doctor who had dedicated himself to country practice where there was a marked shortage of doctors. The mother further wrote that much of the blame should be levelled at the car manufacturer who produced a vehicle that catastrophically crumbled upon impact, killing her daughter.

The letter was my client's "get out of jail free" card and there was little else I needed to say on his behalf. The valiant mother had said it all in her compassionate and insightful letter. The doctor's penalty was non-custodial and he returned to the hospital with his unfortunate memories and commitment to continue practising medicine in the country, hopefully from now on only to save lives.

# Maximum Security Prison

Where in the world can you get free accommodation and all meals provided, free clothes, free medical and dental care, free gym and free cable TV? Not in Bali or Hawaii, but care of Her Majesty's prison system. Many prisoners regard jail-time as a holiday that they can afford; prison supplies every one of their needs except freedom. You could say that prison is a socialist paradise where everything is banned and everyone is equal – apart from the ruling party.

In Fremantle, the port city of Perth, penal convicts built a maximum-security prison that opened in 1855. Fremantle prison was constructed with limestone perimeter walls and crowned in barbwire. The two-storey gatehouse had a façade adorned with a large round clock and the prison was originally built to accommodate one thousand men.

Its four-storey structure featured an austere, 145-metre long, main cellblock. After operating for nearly 140 years, the prison finally locked its gates and ceased operating in 1991 and in 2010 it was listed as a UNESCO World Heritage site and now is a ghoulish tourist destination.

The prison became infamous by virtue of the final execution that took place within its walls, being the hanging of serial murderer Eric Edgar Cooke in 1964. Cooke had terrorised the suburbs of Perth between 1958 and 1963, committing a range of opportunistic crimes including several hit-and-run murders and killing people as they slept or woke to find him an intruder in their homes. He was hanged in the specially constructed gallows room within the bowels of the prison. Imagine being told the actual date and time of your death. It would beg the question: what would you do differently? Unlike the rest of us who wrestle with the metaphysical quandary of our mortality that is certain, yet shrouded in mystery, Eric Cooke knew his date of death, yet ironically, was unable to do anything to change his fate.

Adjoining the main cellblock of the prison is an impressive chapel, which is adorned with four conspicuous wooden boards listing the Ten Commandments. It is no coincidence that our laws largely reflect these commandments and the Judeo-Christian values they espouse. At first glance it might appear odd to have a Christian chapel so prominently positioned in a place such as a prison, where virtues can seem conspicuously absent. Not surprisingly, it has bullet holes in its ceiling and upper walls, caused by various prison riots and skirmishes that occurred over the years. Yet despite all that, it still remained a place of worship for some desperate inmates. It is often the case that a criminal who has stuffed up his or her life – not to mention those of their victims – finds religion and turns to God. The prison chapel is the place where they can seek forgiveness, search for hope and seek redemption from their guilt.

Over the years I have represented a number of serious criminals who have turned to religion in their desperation and sought exoneration from their wrongdoing. In these instances, God becomes their sole means of redemption. Sometimes their faith is founded in genuine remorse, but more often than not it comes from self-pity and sheer regret that they got caught in the first place.

In my early days of legal practice, I recall attending Fremantle Prison to see a client. To do so, I had to book an official visit and comply with prison protocol. This started at the front gate where I underwent a personal security check and then an ID check, before finally being given a visitor's pass. A guard then accompanied me on the walk through the austere quadrangle of the prison and into the wing of the main cellblock. The various gates and doors were unlocked with huge, cumbersome iron keys, which looked like the original keys from 1855, and the gates and doors themselves were the original convict constructions of fortified lumber, limestone and iron that secured each area of the prison. As a young lawyer, I was very impressed with the solemn aspect of the building and its harsh aesthetics. The guards with their rattling keys and gate-opening rituals gave a sense of theatre and grandeur to my experience.

The official interview room had been made by demolishing the dividing wall between two former cells, leaving barely enough room for an interview desk, a couple of chairs and a small cabinet. The walls were adorned with graffiti, and murals that spoke of bygone days and many generations of past criminals. I sat at the table, which was in fact an old wooden school desk. Due to its size, I couldn't get my knees under the desktop, so I sat upright with my legs apart, waiting for my client to be paraded into the cell-come-interview room.

On this occasion my client had been charged with the murder of a policeman in Adelaide. I was advising him as to the merits of his intended objection to the police extradition application that if successful, would see him returned to South Australia for trial. When he walked into the small interview room he cast a shadow over me and the school desk at which I sat, his monstrous frame blocking the light from the solitary bulb that hung from the ceiling, suspended by a single cable. I looked at the hanging light and wondered if this wasn't a bad omen for him. He couldn't fit into the small chair provided, so he stood over the desk glaring down at me. I was wearing a suit and looked every inch the out-of-place lawyer, as he similarly looked every inch the criminal in his prison greens, with dishevelled hair and a straggly beard.

I summoned my courage, greeted him, and began to discuss his case. I told him that I had considered all the documents pertaining to his case and said that in my opinion, there was nothing I could do to help him defeat the extradition application. I told him that unfortunately his objections had no merit and the police would be granted their extradition order that allowed them to take him back to South Australia to face justice. This was not what he wanted to hear. He erupted angrily and screamed at me, calling me a fucking idiot and smashing his fist on the desk so hard that it cracked the flimsy wooden top. He did not have to repeat himself as I clearly understood that he was not happy with my advice or with me.

Due to the commotion, two guards came rushing in. I don't know how they got through the tiny door so quickly, but they somehow squeezed themselves inside and grabbed hold of my client who was still abusing me, and escorted him out of the cell in single file through the same tight door. I heard him still screaming that I was a "fucking idiot" and had "no fucking idea about the law". At that stage I would have been happy to agree with him, and was very relieved to see the back of him. My suit pants had been ripped by splinters of wood from the broken desk, but at least my pants weren't soiled, despite me getting the fright of my life.

After gathering my papers that were now strewn all

over the floor, I regained my composure enough to cautiously make my way out of the interview room and into the open area of the main block. When I got there, the concerned guards enquired after my welfare. I gave a feeble response that understated my terror. As I was leaving the area, I looked up and saw wire netting stretched across the first-floor void of that main block. To change the conversation and distract the guards from my embarrassing incident, I asked them what the wire netting was for. A guard smirked at me and said it was there to catch prisoners when they jump. He continued, saying, "We had one try last night – in fact, it was your client!"

I wish I had known that before my interview with him, as I would have been a lot more sensitive with the delivery of my advice. Unfortunately, on that occasion I left Fremantle Prison having lost a client and a good suit.

# Hot Wheels

High-speed police chases are not uncommon. They generally start with a stolen car being taken for a joy ride, but usually end up rather joyless. I had a client named Rosco who was involved in such a police pursuit after stealing a high-powered Chevrolet Corvette and giving it a run. Whilst speeding on the freeway he came to the attention of an officer in an unmarked police car who immediately gave chase. The officer placed the mobile flashing light on his car roof and activated the hazard lights. In response, my client accelerated so fast that he started to get away, leaving the pursuit vehicle in his wake.

The power of the stolen Corvette was most impressive, and he felt exhilarated. He took the first exit off the Kwinana Freeway in Perth and sped along a side street that took him to a large reserve. It included a dog exercise area where precious pooches could run off the leash. Dominating the landscape was a large lake about one kilometre in diameter. It was well known to the locals for its freshwater crustaceans called yabbies. Rosco was so far in front that he could no longer see the police vehicle, so he abruptly stopped and abandoned the car in the park. He ran furiously, straight towards the lake, where he intended to hide and avoid the police.

He stumbled clumsily to the edge of the lake and took refuge amongst the dense vegetation to avoid detection by the search party, including any hovering police helicopters. From the edge of the lake, he broke a reed that had a hollow centre. The lake was deep in the middle and surrounded by a thick fringe of reeds and tall grasses. He stealthily entered the lake and totally submerged himself, using the reed to breathe through. One end of the reed was in his mouth like a snorkel and the other sat like a periscope above the water. He was well hidden amongst the reeds and grasses of the lake, and was completely invisible.

The pursuit officer had radioed to headquarters the colour and make of the car and asked for assistance. It wasn't long before the abandoned Corvette was found and police arrived to search the park with a tracker K9, the police helicopter and the tactical response group (TRG) – being the Australian equivalent of a SWAT team. Police guessed that my client must have been hiding in or around the lake as there was no other trace of him except for the car, and the police dog couldn't find a scent trail. The vast lake was the obvious place to hide so they positioned the

TRG in different locations around the lake and decided to wait. The other officers returned to their stations.

Rosco remained submerged for over three hours as he waited for nightfall, breathing through the reed and hoping it was not the last straw for him. He later told me that as he crouched in the lake he had to hold the breathing reed with one hand and use the other hand to firmly hold onto the matted roots on the muddy bottom to remain under the water and not float up to the surface. As he stayed there motionless, he could feel leaches attaching themselves to his legs and small fish and crabs nibbling at his exposed skin. His imagination was running rampant and he wondered if it all was worth it. However, he did persist for the remaining few hours until nightfall, when he attempted his escape.

When he thought it was dark enough, he silently emerged from the lake. Rosco was tired, wet, cold and itchy as he stood up in the water, however, his relief was short lived as he was greeted with a bright spotlight emitted from a TRG police vehicle. He was the star of his own show with his own spotlight beaming down on him – as were red lasers from multiple assault rifles. He was arrested on dry land somewhat belatedly and later said to me that the discomfort of the handcuffs paled in comparison to his aquatic ordeal.

Unlike getting away with a joyride in a stolen car, arson must surely be the easiest crime to commit: all you need is a match. Yet it is a serious crime with potentially terminal consequences and so sits high on the scale of criminality. Arson is the unlawful act of wilfully destroying property by fire, the consequences of which can be devastating and fatal, as we hear so often on the news – especially during the Australian summer where bushfires can be catastrophic.

Perhaps because arson is so easy to commit, it seems to attract dull-witted people, or pyromaniacs, or both. Unfortunately for them, the penalty is usually immediate imprisonment and the maximum term as sighted in the Criminal Code is up to 20 years.

In the early 2000s, I represented a twenty-one-year-old man who set fire to a stolen Audi motor vehicle, which he allegedly drove contrary to the stipulations of his learner's permit. It was further alleged that he drove it at high speed when a Ford Territory police patrol vehicle gave chase through the streets of North Perth. During this high-speed chase, the police car with sirens blaring, ran a red light at a busy intersection and slammed into a Toyota Corolla driven by a fifty-year-old woman, killing her instantly and injuring her sixteen-year-old daughter. It was a gang-crime squad officer who had been driving the police pursuit vehicle and he had not been given approval for the high-speed chase. He was subsequently charged with dangerous driving causing death and was stood down from operational duties until his case was resolved. In due course, he was fortunate to be found not guilty by a District Court jury and as a result, returned to his employment.

In a parallel inquiry about the same incident, the deputy state coroner adjudicated that the deceased made a serious error of judgment in assuming that the police car was going to stop at the traffic lights. The coroner was satisfied that the police driver had observed a potential hazard to his left when making his risk assessment, though he had not checked that the Toyota was actually stopping before he continued through the intersection. The inquest focused on police training and the implementation of their emergency driving policy. Whilst it was found that the police driver's action had caused the death of the deceased, it was determined that his actions were undertaken in the course of legitimate law enforcement activities. The coroner further stated that "circumstances such as these require police drivers to make split-second risk assessments with the intent of protecting life and property, while driving a potentially lethal weapon."

After this police chase, which ended dramatically and tragically, my client drove the near-new Audi to a quiet street in East Perth and set it alight using tissues, which he stuffed into the petrol tank. He sprayed perfume, which had been left in the car by its owner, onto the fledgling flames to accelerate the blaze and watched the car burn. He saw the expensive Audi standing proudly before it was enveloped by vertical flames that danced on the black duco and transformed the car into a mess of metal and plastic behind pluming acrid smoke. The fire was so impressive that my client took a photo of it with his mobile phone. He then left the scene, ran down the road and called a taxi.

He was later arrested and charged with arson. The allegations against him were that during the police pursuit he had seen the dramatic collision in his rear-view mirror and fearing the worst, he torched the Audi in an attempt to destroy any link between himself and the police pursuit that had culminated in a fatality.

During sentencing, the Supreme Court judge heard from me as defence counsel that my client was a recovering drug addict whose addiction had reached crisis point in the weeks leading up to the torching of the Audi. Burning that car had been his futile attempt to hide his involvement, though ironically, in doing so had drawn attention to the vehicle and subsequently brought about his arrest. His Honour sentenced my client in relation to the crime of arson, to a term of four years imprisonment, and the associated traffic offences carried a further custodial sentence of 19 months. The judge also fined my client $200 and disqualified him from driving for the 12 months following his release from jail.

Ironically, it was the photo that my client had taken of the burning Audi that incriminated him in the arson charge. When I asked him why he had taken the photo and kept this damning evidence on his phone, he told me that as he was walking away from the scene, he looked back at the burning car and thought it was so spectacular he had to take a photo of it for prosperity. At the end of the day, justice was served: he did not get to frame the photo, but he did frame himself.

On a lighter note, I recall watching the television news one evening in which a report appeared of a fire that had totally destroyed a house. I recognised the man being interviewed about the blaze as a previous client of mine, a South American man whose name, memorably, was Jesus. He was a tenant of the house with some other ex-cons. He was filmed standing in front of the burnt-out house wearing a grubby singlet and stubbies with a beer in his hand. He was still sporting his iconic monobrow and a brushtail beard, and even though the interview was impromptu and the circumstances grim, Jesus was smiling broadly, pleased to be on television. The interviewer was priming a scoop as to how the fire might have started and after speaking to the police asked Jesus the leading question, "I understand there was a cannabis bong in the house. Could that have caused the fire?"

Jesus retorted indignantly, "I doubt it! What house doesn't have a bong?"

# Violence Against Women

Kevin was a homeless forty-five-year-old. He wasn't a victim of the recession or the downturn in the global economy, he was simply a loser. He embarked on a criminal career from an early age and his downfall was of his own making. He had criminal convictions in New South Wales, Victoria, South Australia, Queensland and now Western Australia; his transient lifestyle was determined by the outstanding arrest warrants he had across Australia. He tried to be one step ahead of the law and when an arrest warrant was issued to him for pending criminal charges, he would simply move to another state of Australia. He could move quickly as he had no assets or valuables to worry about. He simply packed his backpack and went on the road hitchhiking between the states and utilising the charity of others.

Kevin was a chronic alcoholic and spent most of his dole money on alcohol. His life's mantra revolved around grog and it was not quality but quantity that he was after. He had struggled with this disease for over 30 years and accepted his unfortunate plight in life. With no fewer than three outstanding arrest warrants in other states, Kevin materialised in Perth, and set up a humpy in bushland neighbouring a golf course on the outskirts of the city. The humpy was no more than a crude lean-to that would suffice as his temporary home.

Any real estate agent will tell you that with property, location is everything – the slogan "location, location, location" says it all. Well, Kevin's bush humpy was no different. It was on prime land and had everything that he needed, being situated near a Liquorland, Centrelink and the TAB. Despite the great location, he didn't have any visitors and in fact didn't want visitors, as the only people that might come around would be the police.

Dole day came around each second Thursday and his money would appear in his bank account at the ATM a few minutes past midnight. Kevin withdrew the dole cash as quickly as his tiny fat fingers would allow. His personal budget permitted him a little cash for some cheap fast food and the essential cigarettes, and the rest of it would be spent on booze. Obviously, his budget did not need to allow for land rates and taxes despite the prime location of the humpy.

Kevin was not a handsome man. He was short and

stocky, his face bore the signs of many years of alcohol abuse and his eyes squinted from constant cigarette smoke and exposure to the elements. An unpleasant odour emanated from him warning others that he hadn't showered for weeks. His general appearance was that of a hobo and in fact that is exactly what he was.

During one of his visits to the nearby ATM, Kevin met a homeless woman who was a lot younger, only twenty years old, and who was also in dire straits. He invited her for a drink, not at the nearby hotel as she hoped, but to his bush humpy. She was already very drunk at the time – as she was most of the time – and so she went with him. She was vulnerable but was happy to source another drink from him.

As soon as they arrived at the well located humpy, he plied her with alcohol. It was very cheap wine and there was lots of it, as it was only one day after dole day and he had stocked up. It didn't take him long to ask her for sex. He was obviously hoping that she was drunk enough to find him desirable and would say yes. However, no amount of alcohol was sufficient to make her drunk enough that she didn't find him repulsive. She rejected his advances, but he was insistent, and started to get violent towards her. He was going to have sex with his guest with or without her consent. She claimed that as she tried to deny him, he smashed her head into the ground, punched her in the face and choked her into submission. Kevin then allegedly raped her as she lay distressed and motionless on the ground.

He held her captive for three days and nights using a combination of cable ties and alcohol to confine her. During these days of her detention and his depravity, he repeatedly raped her and sexually assaulted her. When she tried to escape, he violently attacked her again and again – depriving her of her liberty and dignity. On the fourth day, while Kevin was sleeping in a drunken stupor, his victim escaped from the bush humpy that had been her house of horrors. She sought help and received medical treatment for her facial and other injuries at the local hospital. The police were called to hear her surreal story.

After being charged with rape, deprivation of liberty and assault, Kevin pleaded not guilty to all the charges and subsequently stood trial before a judge and jury in the Supreme Court. At trial, the young woman, who had previously been a homeless vagrant, had, with the help of the victim support team, transformed herself into a sober and credible young witness who convincingly articulated her ordeal to the jury. Kevin on the other hand, having elected to give evidence in his defence, gave a disjointed narrative lacking all credibility that was rejected by the jury. He was, unsurprisingly, convicted of all charges.

In preparing my sentencing submissions for and on behalf of Kevin, I was desperate to find some mitigating factors about his life and character that I could beneficially present to the Court. His personal antecedence and long criminal record were negative factors and unhelpful for seeking a lenient sentence. I was keen to show the Court that he was more than just an opportunistic rapist who lived in a bush humpy.

I asked him if he could tell me something about his life that showed some stability and commitment. All of sudden his face lit up and he said to me, "What about me being married for twelve years and having six children?" I chirped with glee, saying, "Yes! That's exactly what I need to hear. Tell me about this long and stable marriage with six children." He replied, "Oh yeah, but it wasn't one marriage. It was to four different women, and I haven't seen any of the kids."

I shook my head in disbelief. At the end of the day I had little to say on his behalf. Kevin was sentenced to a total of seven years jail and was moved to his new location. His new accommodation was far more secure, as well as dry, warm and comfortable with a bed, a roof and three meals a day.

Unfortunately, the physical and sexual violence Kevin perpetrated against the young woman is all too common, and violence against women can sometimes escalate to murder, particularly in a domestic relationship.

Curtains in the home can provide privacy from the outside world and prying eyes. Bedroom curtains act as a visual barrier and come in all shapes and sizes to suit their purpose. A curtain in a bedroom can shield one from the outside world, unless there is someone hiding behind it with a hammer in hand and an evil intent. Curtains are still used in some cinemas and theatres where they open evocatively to introduce the action, but in the following story, the curtains in the victim's home hid a villain straight out of a horror movie.

Martin and Maria's wedding day was joyful, as were the first six years of their married life. However, as time went on, Martin struggled to make ends meet and Maria had to work as a schoolteacher to help out. She came from a close-knit Italian family who held many family socials and revelled in the traditions of their homeland. Maria was very well liked as a person and respected as a dedicated teacher. She and Martin were looking forward to buying a house they could call their own and then start a family.

Martin was considered a little strange by his wife's extended family and these criticisms got back to him. Martin felt ostracised by his in-laws, though he accepted the label of "strange" as he knew he was different from others. This difference had not been diagnosed as a mental illness, it was more of a behavioural issue, demonstrated by his obsessive character, which sometimes saw him succumb to uncontrolled emotions of jealousy, rage and lust. His strangeness contrasted with, and was highlighted by, his wife's sweet temperament and popularity.

The pressure upon their marriage became unbearable and Martin began to threaten his wife with violence during the last months of their relationship. Maria, in response, obtained a violence restraining order (a VRO) against Martin at the Perth Magistrate's Court – in effect, restraining him from approaching her and/or entering the family home to which she was given exclusive use. He was enraged with the court order that had barred him from his own home and property. He couldn't accept the humiliation that his wife was causing him. He was sure that her family was behind it all and he hated them all. The perceived unfairness of her actions infuriated him. He decided that he wasn't going to take this treatment lying down and would fight back. He regarded the VRO as nothing more than a piece of paper and it was not going to shield her from his revenge.

For the previous 20 years, Martin's adult criminal record characterised him as being a serious nuisance, a stalker and a danger to women. In the past, he had breached many VROs obtained by an ex-girlfriend and his behaviour had resulted in convictions of unlawful entry, serious threats and several assaults.

Knowing his current wife's work habits and movements, one afternoon while she was still at work, Martin unlawfully gained entry into the former matrimonial home by removing roof tiles and dropping through a manhole in the ceiling. On his way into the main part of the house he passed through the garage and grabbed a hammer. This was a wooden-handled, steel-headed hammer that he had previously used to nail loose fence boards together.

The inside of the house that was well known to him was silent and stark. He made his way from the laundry door, which he carefully closed and locked, through the lounge and past the kitchen table he had bought two years before. He passed the spare room and moved into the main bedroom that he and his wife had used intimately during their previous happy times. The bedroom was dominated by a king-size bed and heavy, full-length curtains. These curtains covered the large windows and rested on the soft, carpeted floor.

It wasn't long before Maria came home from work. As she came in through the front door Martin hid behind the bedroom curtains. He stood there with his back against the window and face in the curtain holding the hammer in his preferred hand. He was beyond talking and now it was time for action. He stood there very forlorn and dejected as his wife had the law and family on her side. He remained in situ for nearly three hours while Maria had dinner, watched some television with her dog Sally and finally went to bed. Martin's ability to stand still for such a long time seems extraordinary when one considers how long it feels to stand at attention for a two-minute silence or for the microwave to heat a meal. Anyway, he stood there in his solitude with his evil intentions waiting for Maria to fall asleep so he could attack her.

All this time Maria had no idea there was someone in her bedroom, let alone her deranged husband with a hammer in his hand and thoughts of revenge. She closed the bedroom door as she did every night to keep Sally out. Sally was a gorgeous King Charles Cavalier spaniel, a small breed of dog with a wonderful temperament. She had been given Sally by her auntie just weeks before, to keep her company during the acrimonious bust-up with Martin. The dog was good company when she was home and gave her comfort during this trying period.

When Martin was sure that Maria was asleep, he crept out from behind the curtain and approached the bed. While she lay there, asleep and defenceless, he lifted the hammer and bashed her head many times with it. He then dropped the hammer and grabbed her throat with both hands, choking the last breath from her body. He stopped his cowardly attack only to have oral, anal and vaginal intercourse whilst she was unconscious and dying. Blood had soaked into the satin pillow and white sheets. Blood spatter covered the wall and bedhead in a deadly mosaic. For some inconceivable reason, he then dragged her limp body into the en-suite shower and bathed her. No one knows what he was saying to her, if anything. It was all too late for the poor victim who would no longer teach or enjoy her family. After the shower, he partly dried her and placed her lifeless body on the bed that he had hastily rearranged. On his own admission, he then committed necrophilia.

His self-gratification and revenge were fulfilled in this most villainous and morbid way. Her dog was of no interest to him, but was barking loudly outside the bedroom door and was annoying him. Sally was distracting him from his fatal mission, and so he decided to deal with this nuisance. Without hesitation, he opened the bedroom door where Sally was barking and struck her head with the bloodied hammer. It only took one stroke and Sally collapsed at his feet no longer barking but now whimpering her last breath. Having murdered his wife of six years, he then stole her car and drove away. Soon after, he became overwhelmed by guilt and telephoned the police announcing to them his heinous crime. Later he gave a full confession and cooperated with the police investigation. His actions rendered the violence restraining order meaningless and not worth the paper on which it was written, as in this case, the barred person had total disregard for the law.

At my first meeting with Martin, just days after he was arrested and held in custody on remand, I tried to discuss with him the salient aspects of his deplorable actions, but I didn't get far because he was crying and sobbing hysterically. I thought he was upset for himself so I tried to lift his spirits with some casual words of comfort, those being, "Hang in there Martin, these troubles will pass with time." He looked up at me with bloodshot, teary eyes and said, "It's alright for you to say that, but I'm still grieving." This preposterous comment astounds me to this day.

When his charges came before the Supreme Court, he did not contest them but pleaded guilty to the crimes of gaining unauthorised entry into the home, breaching the restraining order, killing the dog and murdering his wife. The charges of aggravated sexual penetration were dropped by the state prosecutor because it was their opinion that in the scheme of things, pursuing such additional charges was not in the public interest. At sentencing, the judge eloquently said that the unfortunate day Maria had answered Martin's advertisement through an internet dating agency was "the day that she signed her own death warrant. That was the fatal day that she let into her life someone who was manipulative, controlling, violent and obsessive." His violent actions demonstrated his utter contempt for his wife who at that stage was nothing more than an object of his lust and he showed utter contempt for the violence restraining order. Martin received a life sentence with a considerable minimum of 27 years imprisonment to serve before he could be eligible for parole. This was one of the longest minimum terms ever imposed for murder in Western Australia.

I assume that after serving, at least, the minimum period of 27 years Martin would have had sufficient time to stop grieving.

# The Burlesque Vegetable Show

The primal instincts of humans designed to ensure self-preservation and procreation are directed towards the four basic needs for food, physical security, sex and social relationships. Oddly enough, the local hotel can provide for all these needs, but of course the question of physical security depends on the level of inebriation.

I represented a husband and wife, once, who had been charged for disorderly conduct by behaving in an indecent manner in a public place, namely the lounge bar of a prominent hotel in Perth. They performed a highly suggestive dance and mime act as part of the hotel's lunchtime lingerie show and pleaded not guilty to the charge of public indecency. This meant the police prosecutor had to prove the elements of the charge beyond reasonable doubt to the presiding magistrate. During the trial, the prosecutor attempted to prove the charge to the required standard of proof by calling witnesses who he hoped would satisfy the magistrate that the act was indecent. In other words, the allegation was that the act was offensive, against the recognised standards of decency in our society.

One such witness for the prosecution was a thirty-year-old male primary school teacher who said in his evidence, that during the act there was a dance routine that involved the man (who happened to be the husband) laying on top of the woman (his wife), simulating sexual intercourse. This witness continued his testimony by saying, on oath, that the dance contained a lot of suggestive movements and concluded with the woman pulling a carrot out of the front of the man's trousers and proceeding to eat it. The teacher said that the carrot was clearly a stand-in for the man's penis. He continued his complaint by saying that he found the performance pointless, unnecessary and rude. As defence counsel for the accused couple, I sat there listening to his drivel and couldn't help but feel sorry for the poor students this self-righteous teacher was supposedly educating.

Another male prosecution witness was a twenty-nine-year-old electrician who told the Court that he found the show disgusting and rude. However, the lingerie show that followed, in which young women paraded themselves around in see-through underwear, he said he had found quite tasteful. In fact, he told the Court that he had seen my clients' act no fewer than three times and had complained to the police each time.

In this instance, I was able to act for both defendants, as there was no conflict of interest in representing them together. In their defence, the husband and wife gave evidence on oath, stating that they carefully choreographed their routine to suit the audience that was attracted to the girly lingerie show. They were genuine artists, they said, and had the ability to suggest actions without actually performing them. Theirs was a burlesque show that titillated the audience with simulated sexual interaction between a male and a female. In defending them I submitted that their performance had to be considered in its context: presented to an adult audience who had come to see a bogus fashion parade that was nothing more than a risqué girly show of women in see-through lingerie. My clients' show not only complemented the "fashion parade", but also promoted the carrot as a superfood. I submitted that their show was burlesque but not indecent. Unsurprisingly the magistrate acquitted the husband and wife of the ridiculous charge and ruled that while their dance and mime was highly suggestive, it was not indecent.

Though my clients were cleared of indecency, they chose to never again perform that act, so consequently the electrician witness could not see them perform for the fourth time. For that matter, I guess the young teacher never ate a carrot again.

# A Chip Off the Old Block

The sun rose as it did every day over the wheat fields of Katanning, a town of about 4,000 people in the Wheatbelt region some 250km south-east of Perth. Joel was an Aboriginal resident of the town and had been out of work for many years. On an autumn morning in 1993, Joel and his nine-year-old son were having vegemite on toast for breakfast. He was grateful for the fortnightly welfare payments he was receiving from the government and it was cheaper to live in the country, out of the expensive city. That was why he was able to afford to buy a near-new Holden Monaro GTS that was his pride and joy. The Monaro was a powerful coupe with a V8 HEMI engine and dual gold racing stripes running up the centre of the bonnet over the British racing green duco. It had mag wheels and high-performance tyres and was fitted with a loud exhaust that amplified the engine sound so as to let the town folk know that Joel was coming. The town of Katanning had a single main road that at times became the drag strip for his hot Monaro, depending upon his mood. Unsurprisingly, Joel and the car were well known to the local police.

That morning, while things were quiet in town, Joel took his son for a spin in the Monaro. Outside of town the roads were long and connected to other nearby towns and farms. These roads were mostly traversed by the locals as well as the trucks that transported cereal crops to bulk grain centres. Joel's son was also christened Joel, as at the time of his birth, his father couldn't think of a more befitting name than his own. Unwittingly, Joel Junior became known simply as "Junior", not "Joel" as his father had intended. He was, however, the clone of his father and lived full-time with him as his mother had abandoned him when he was three years old. She went off with another fella leaving Junior and the town behind.

Joel and Junior took to the road with much noise and speed. The announcement was heard by the local police and what ensued quickly became a high-speed police chase along the road to the nearby town. When the police approached from behind, they flashed their lights at him to stop the car. But instead of stopping, Joel put his foot to the floor and the Monaro's revving V8 responded by thrusting the car forward at high speed. The police-issue Holden Commodore had trouble keeping up and alerted nearby patrol cars to assist in the pursuit. Before long there were four police cars in hot pursuit of Joel who was travelling in excess of 180km/h.

After thirty or so minutes, in the distant horizon and on the crest of the road, Joel saw another three police cars approaching from afar. Fearing a roadblock, he instinctively took a road to the left, which had presented itself at that opportune moment. The Monaro slid sideways but fortunately the four tyres kept it on the road and gravel verge. Without warning, however, that side road was a dead-end, blocked by a locked farm gate. The police cars with sirens blaring all converged upon him. Not only did they park the cars across the road, trapping the Monaro, a total of six officers jumped out and like in a movie scene, stood alongside each other with their service revolvers drawn and pointing at the Monaro that had spun 180 degrees and was now facing them.

Joel's adrenaline was pumping, and in that moment, his only intention was to drive through the police roadblock. He had the car and audacity to do it. This was not his first police chase and hopefully it would not be his last, though he was effectively facing a firing squad. Neither Joel nor Junior were wearing seatbelts. Joel could see what was coming, so he barked at Junior to get down on the passenger floor. Junior curled up like a human ball, tucking his knees up against his small chest and wrapped his long arms around them. As Joel revved the engine and started to come at the police blockade, the police opened fire on the car. The Monaro drove through the police rank as some officers dived aside to allow the car to go through. The Monaro was hit by no fewer than twenty-three bullets. Junior's diminutive figure was most vulnerable to serious, if not fatal, injuries from the barrage of gunfire and bullets ricocheting throughout the car. Joel himself was shot in the leg, arm and waist, which were not fatal injuries, but surprisingly, Junior was completely unscathed. The human ball survived the frightening ordeal.

I was defence counsel at the trial, which was held before a judge and jury in a nearby regional town. Joel, who now was my client, was defending six counts of attempted murder of those six policemen who were involved in the blockade and shootout. It was alleged that my client used his powerful car to attempt to kill the officers who were going about their lawful duty. The defence was that Joel had no intention of killing or harming any of the six officers; he simply wanted to get out of the firing range and so drove accordingly. The officers on the road, who had to jump out of the Monaro's way, had put themselves in that position.

In the first week of the long trial, the prosecutor presented to the jury a model representing the direction of each bullet and position of each bullet hole, by using three-metre dowelling rods stuck in each of the twenty-three bullet holes. The Monaro looked like a porcupine, though ironically, the spikes of this porcupine would not prick holes in the defence. One of the astounding facts of the case was that Junior had not been hit by any of the bullets, whose trajectories were illustrated in court by the porcupine configuration of bullet holes. They encircled, but luckily did not touch, the human ball. Fortunately for Junior, he had faced a firing squad of bad shots. Mind you, there was no evidence suggesting that any of the police officers knew that Junior was in the car.

During the second week of trial, my client fell asleep in court. Not only was he asleep in the dock before the judge and jury, he was also snoring and had his feet up on the balustrade. The judge indignantly stopped proceedings and asked a guard to wake my client. He awoke startled and loudly exclaimed, "Shit!" His Honour explained to him that he should be paying attention, that these were serious charges and he should stay awake, to which my client retorted, "Judge, I've got my lawyer, and I don't understand nothin' anyway." The jury had a giggle and His Honour repeated himself to the accused, emphasising the importance of staying awake.

Joel was very awake for the jury verdict, however, which was one of not guilty for each of the six charges of attempted murder. The jury accepted that he was merely trying to evade capture. He was subsequently dealt with in a lower court for the high-speed pursuit and associated traffic charges, to which he pleaded guilty, and for which he received a short period in custody.

The old time saying "like father, like son" proved true in this case as some twelve years later I received an in-struction from Joel Junior, also on a charge of attempted murder, requesting that I represent him. I was very pleased to oblige him.

The expression "like father, like son" is not exclusive to the male gender however, it also manifests itself in the maternal line as "like mother, like daughter". Some years ago, I had the dubious privilege of representing a young woman who adorned herself with tattoos and facial piercings. She had no time for lipstick and make up but had spent a lot of time getting neck and face tattoos. Her neck bore an image of a two-headed snake, the body of which was wrapped around the back of the neck and the two heads were poised beneath her ears. I was reluctant to ask my client what this tattoo meant, and in fact made no mention of any of her tattoos, nor the nose and lip piercings, during any of our interviews. I pretended that it was all normal – which it wasn't – and continued with the consultation.

As if her appearance was not bad enough, I suddenly noticed her chewing her tongue between her comments to me. This chewing was obvious – like a cow chewing its cud. You could see the full roll of the mouth and the yellow teeth. Even her facial jewellery, if you could call the bits of tin and baubles "jewellery", moved in unison with her chewing. There was a lot happening with her face as she gave me her full instructions. In fact, the distraction was so great that I have forgotten the substance of her problem, but I do remember that it involved illicit drugs.

Later, I convinced the sentencing judge that she shouldn't be imprisoned because she had a baby daughter to look after. Fortunately for her, the court exercised leniency and let her be a mother rather than a prisoner.

Many years later, she came to see me again, but this time with her now grown daughter who was in trouble with the law. The years had not been kind to the mother. Her face drooped and was no longer adorned with baubles nor piercings and the faded snake tattoo was hibernating in the folds of her wrinkled skin. The daughter was no oil painting either but at least she had no piercings or visible tattoos. After short introductions, I turned to the daughter to ask about her problem, but before she said anything she started to chew her tongue just like her mother had. It all came back to me. "Oh my God!" I thought. "Like mother, like daughter".

It must be said that people are all different, but I have found in my criminal practice that some are more different than others.

# The Lotto Winners

In the early years of my legal practice, I had many Polish clients as I spoke the language fluently – more so then than now. During this time in the early 80s, there were about 14,000 Poles in Perth who had come after being displaced from Poland after the Second World War. They would stream into my office, especially for Family Court matters. It was often a race to the door as to which spouse could engage me first, forcing the other to use a non-Polish speaking lawyer.

One Monday morning, I arrived at my office at about 7:30am and was hurriedly met by my first Polish client for the day. She did not have an appointment but said it was extremely urgent that I see her. She had been waiting at the front door for at least an hour. Her story began with her and her husband sponsoring her mother to come from Poland for a six-month holiday. While they only had a small, rented apartment, it was still salubrious for the mother who had lived an austere life in Poland and had very little to her name.

When she arrived the mother became fascinated by the idea of lotto and couldn't believe the size of the prize money that could be won each week – how one could become a millionaire overnight. There was nothing like it in Poland. Lotto was a fairytale dream for her, something that could transform her rags into riches. During the first week of her stay, the mother had written out the birth dates of all three of them and started playing lotto. The agreement was that each of them would contribute a third of the cost of the ticket and she, her daughter and her son-in-law would likewise share into three any winnings that came their way. This arrangement went on for a couple of months.

However, as time passed, the daughter and son-in-law became tardy in paying their weekly contribution for the lotto tickets. Maybe they thought they didn't need to keep contributing to the mother's fantasy, thinking they had no chance of winning. The mother ended up paying the whole amount each week, but her resolve was unshaken and her determination to give herself every chance of becoming a millionaire remained.

Then, one Saturday night, the daughter and son-in-law were preparing dinner while the mother sat glued to the television watching the lotto draw for that week. The kitchen was in the same open-plan area where the television had pride of place. The two could see the mother sitting on the lounge holding the lotto ticket. She didn't really need the ticket to remember the weekly numbers, as they were personally significant and imprinted in her mind. When the first four numbers were drawn, mirroring exactly the ticket she was holding, she started screaming with delight, "Chodź! Chodź! Chodź!" which was Polish for "Come! Come! Come!" By the time the fifth and sixth numbers were read out – and also matched her ticket – she was in hysterics.

All of a sudden, the mother had the full attention of all those present. The elated daughter moved from the kitchen to the lounge to embrace her mother, as her husband rushed past her and plucked the winning ticket from his mother-in-law's hand like a bird of prey and disappeared into the bedroom, locking the door behind him. The mother and daughter were still jumping with delight as he was jumping out of the scene. He hastily packed some clothes and personal belongings into a flimsy suitcase and came out of the bedroom announcing that he and the lotto ticket were leaving. He left the house with the mother and his wife dumbfounded and shocked; their joy turned to disbelief and disgust. There was no sight or sound of him for the rest of the weekend. He didn't even go to church on Sunday!

His greed obviously overwhelmed all his other values and attributes. After all, this was a lotto jackpot win of $5 million. He must have thought at the time that winning the jackpot was worth more than his relationship with his wife and any respect he had for his mother-in-law. That was the gist of the instructions I received that early Monday morning and it was urgent indeed. I sprang into action at about the same speed as the husband had left his home. There was no time to waste as the husband could have claimed the prize that morning from Lottery West. I prepared an urgent affidavit, the client's sworn testimony of what happened, and filed it with the Supreme Court of Western Australia together with an application for an injunction seeking an order to stop the Lotto payment being made to the husband.

I alerted the manager of Lottery West that urgent legal action had been initiated and asked him to delay processing the prize money until I could serve the injunction on Lottery West later that morning – as soon as I got the court order. The manager advised me that the husband was already in the premises claiming the $5 million. He had the ticket and there were no other winners in that division to share the jackpot. The manager agreed to stall things to allow the court process to take its course.

I promptly attended the Supreme Court with my client and documents. Surprisingly, though perhaps understandably, the mother herself did not attend my office or the Court hearing. At the hearing you could see bemusement on the judge's face when he read the documents and subsequently ordered the injunction. I personally served the injunction order on Lottery West and fortunately stopped the payment of the $5 million to the husband. We now had time to resolve the issues in an orderly and fair manner. I did not think the question of whether the three of them would share the winnings was in issue, as I expected that the husband and wife would both agree with the mother to a one-third share each.

In the following week it became evident that the mother had in fact paid for the whole cost of the lotto ticket and had not received any contribution from her daughter or son-in-law. It was therefore legally arguable that the mother had won the money for herself, by herself, and didn't need to share it. I never saw the mother, nor was she a client of mine such that I would advise her. It transpired that the daughter and son-in-law reconciled their marriage and apparently agreed with the mother that they would take $4.75 million and the mother would get $250,000 and "fuck off back to Poland".

It's amazing how a Supreme Court injunction can re-kindle the love and devotion between a husband and wife. Unfortunately for the mother, though, there was a lot less love and devotion afforded her.

# Tropical Murder

While some try to run off with $5 million, others have more modest amounts in their sights, and unfortunately for Jack, his grab for a miserable $14 cost him his life. It happened in the Kimberley town of Kununurra in Western Australia. The area is famous for its ancient rugged beauty and for its diamonds. Jack and his missus called Wendy had been separated for many months after a relatively long relationship of six years and he now lived well out of town. Though he didn't frequent the town very often, when he did, he would always seek out his ex-missus to bum some money off her or ask for a favour. Wendy knew this well and was the more capable person of the two. She was a thirty-eight-year-old Aboriginal woman, and was somewhat overweight and sickly. She enjoyed being single again and had a close-knit group of friends. She had no need for him and was fairing very well on her own, despite suffering from diabetes and a serious heart condition. Her life was simple and revolved around her carefree friends and the card games they played on the verandah during the hot tropical evenings.

This late afternoon, Wendy was playing cards and socialising with some family and friends. It was a game in which they placed small bets to make it more interesting. She was one of four seated at a cheap laminex table on the verandah of a friend's house. She had her meagre winnings of $14 sitting on the table next to her discarded cards, when out of thin air Jack appeared. He walked up to Wendy and without warning or greeting grabbed her cash, proclaiming it was now his and that he was taking it. At first, she was astonished by his unexpected appearance and then astounded by his bullying. She reacted spontaneously and grabbed for his hand, trying to recover the cash from his grip. He resisted and as she got up, grappling him for the cash, they both fell off the verandah where they continued to wrestle on the unkempt lawn.

Jack was slightly shorter than Wendy and was very drunk at the time. While they were rolling on the lawn, Wendy saw Jack reach out for a rock and thought that he would club her with it. She let go of him and broke his hold of her. This allowed her to get up and return to the card table where her handbag lay by her fallen chair. She reached into her bag and produced a small, serrated vegetable knife, which she normally used to cut meat and vegetables in the kitchen. She had brought it on this occasion to help with her friend's dinner preparation. Wendy grabbed the knife, returned to the lawn, moved towards Jack and while facing him, thrust it into his heart. Later, her explanation was that she thought he was behind her with the rock and she feared for her life. This suggested a classic case of self-defence except for the fact that she had the knife and he had only a rock. Unfortunately for her, the evidence suggested that he wasn't behind her at all, but that she had turned to him with the knife and done him in.

She never got her $14 back, but instead swapped it for 14 years minimum jail on a life sentence for murder.

It is somewhat eerie for me to recall that during recess in this trial's proceedings, I was approached by the auntie of my client. She told me that on the morning of the murder, she had a strong premonition of her niece killing someone. She felt such disquiet that she even told my client about it before the evening card game but unfortunately no heed was given to the premonition, and fate took its course.

# Australia's Most Useless Bank Robbers II

The glory days of bank bandits who used balaclavas and shotguns were in the period leading up to the 1990s when banks still held large amounts of cash and hadn't yet implemented the security of time-delayed safes, high-definition cameras, safety glass and so on. In those days, bank robbers resembled the likes of the Ned Kelly gang and their weapon of choice was usually the sawn-off shotgun. Revolvers and pistols were harder to get and were not as confronting and scary as the double-barrel shotgun. With two thirds of the barrel and most of its stock sawn off, it was short enough to hide in a carry bag or behind a coat, yet still be intimidating – and deadly.

A complete shotgun in its untampered form would be used on a farm or at a clay target club. The full barrel of the shotgun allowed the projectiles to stay grouped for longer as they left the barrel, unlike the sawn-off shotgun, which sprayed the projectiles from its very short barrel. While a farmer, for example, used the full barrel to shoot at vermin some 50 metres away, a bank robber only needed a short barrel to shoot at a target a few metres away. The robber would, and sometimes still did, disguise himself by wearing a balaclava, a garment covering the whole head and neck except for the eyes and mouth. Gloves were also worn so as not to leave fingerprints. The moneybag, of course, was compulsory as was the gruff announcement, "This is a stick up."

I represented one such robber who boldly burst into a bank wearing his balaclava and gloves and armed with a loaded, double-barrel, sawn-off 12-gauge shotgun. It was just minutes before closing time and the bank tellers were thinking of getting ready to go home when their world was rudely disrupted by this armed bandit. He stood in the middle of the foyer shouting, "This is a robbery! Hand over all your cash." The first response to his demand was shock and disbelief. One teller ducked below the counter while the other two stood in terror. To emphasise his demand, the robber pulled the trigger and discharged a cartridge from one barrel into the ceiling. However, instead of adding emphasis, the ceiling came crashing down upon him.

He was covered by many years' worth of rubble and dust as the bank occupied a quaint heritage building dating back to the previous century. It was located in the town of Guildford, an early settlement of the Swan River colony and now a suburb of Perth. The debris that fell on the robber made him look like Ned Kelly's ghost. With dust in his eyes and nothing more to say, he turned and ran outside but instead of running through the front door from which he'd came, he crashed through the plate glass window adjoining the door. Shards of glass fell and encapsulated him. Because of the balaclava, layers of clothes and gloves he was wearing, he didn't get cut by the glass, but his ego was certainly bruised – more so than the bruises he received from slipping and falling onto the broken glass.

As the robber lay sprawled on the pavement outside the bank, shotgun still in hand and holding onto his empty moneybag, some bystanders sprang into action and effected a citizen's arrest. A citizen's arrest is the power that an ordinary citizen has in detaining a person who has just committed or is committing an offence. The citizen has no power to search or do anything to the offender other than use reasonable force to detain them until they can be presented to the police. There is an obvious risk associated with making a citizen's arrest: not only is one exposed to the risk of physical harm to oneself, but one also takes on a duty of care to the detainee who is now under their control and power. In this case, the citizens acted reasonably when they overpowered the robber before he could flee the scene. The bank was a mess, as was the robber's plan, however he'd been nicked, which clearly wasn't. The commotion of the robbery only took a few minutes but its impact upon the tellers and witnesses would unfortunately last a lifetime.

When justice finally caught up with the failed armed robber, he received six years imprisonment and was ordered to pay significant damages for repairing the ceiling and glass window. Upon the conclusion of proceedings, I was well aware that he had no ability to pay for the substantial repairs and I had little doubt that he would, in due course, need to revert to the "banking business".

On a more recent occasion, I represented a far more successful bank robber who had managed to steal over $5,000, but in the end wasn't totally successful, as he eventually got caught. Rod was a career criminal. From an early age he started collecting convictions at a great rate. His Children's Court record was appalling and his lengthy jail time as a juvenile prepared him well for the career he chose as an adult.

At thirty-three years of age, Rod's criminal record boasted over 100 convictions contained in 11 pages of approximately 10 convictions per page. He had spent more than half of his life in the care of Her Majesty's prison, where he got three regular meals, a cosy cell, and gym and work out yard, in which he kept himself fit and strong. His physical qualities, together with the education he received from his cellmates, put him in good stead to maintain his adult career as a criminal.

It was inside cellblock A that he and his mates would conjure up different scenarios of robbing banks. There was a certain bravado amongst the inmates when they talked about holding up banks, and they reasoned that the bank had enough money to give away. They bragged about their own exploits and regarded the armed robber as a tough dude; doing the crime was a macho gig, just like doing the time. They gave little thought and had no empathy for the collateral damage caused to the victims and witnesses of their crimes. Criminals such as Rod built their careers on self-gratification and a total disregard for others.

The courts described Rod as a sociopath: a person who doesn't respect laws or social norms and doesn't feel guilt or remorse for actions that harm others. Rod's deviance from society was often violent, but fortunately he was not a sexual predator. His preoccupation was solely on what he could get for himself without being caught. One might say that modern-day punishment is too soft and allows criminals to keep reoffending and never learn their lesson. Maybe the professional industry of social workers, psychologists, judges and lawyers etc. has a vested interest in the revolving doors of recidivism so as to maintain their careers.

When Rod was on parole in 1988 for a spate of frauds

for which he originally received two years jail, he decided to hatch the plan of an armed bank robbery. He had mulled it over for a few months whilst in custody and been able to receive expert advice from a serial bank robber who shared his cell. This "expert" advised Rod of the six cardinal rules of armed bank robbery which were: study the bank; time the entry; uncover the firearm; point it at a teller; impact the scene; and depart the bank quickly. This advice sounds great until one realises that the acronym spells out STUPID.

Rod, however, was undeterred in his quest to rob the bank. He organised his gloves and some unassuming dark clothes. He couldn't get a balaclava at short notice, so he had no option but to use a full-face helmet, which he stole off a parked motorbike. With all the apparel in place he needed to source a firearm. Much to his delight, a previous accomplice provided him with an old sawn-off shotgun that looked as if it had been waved in a bank before. Rod wanted to borrow the shotgun but his mate wouldn't hear of it and insisted he buy it for $100. He explained that he had no money and that was the reason why he needed to do the robbery. They agreed that Rod would pay twice the price, from the bank proceeds. There was no discussion about getting shotgun cartridges as Rod already told his mate that he had no money. Rod would have to pretend that it was loaded, and, in any event, the sawn-off shotgun looked lethal. The handgrip was barely there right next to the firing mechanism, and the two short barrels just protruded from the wooden stock. The firearm was menacing in appearance and just right for the job at hand. Rod assumed it wouldn't be necessary to shoot off a round in order to gain the attention and compliance of the bank tellers; the appearance of the shotgun was sufficiently intimidating.

Rod mentally rehearsed the robbery many times and was sure it would go down smoothly. He had been to the chosen bank a few times before and staked it out. His plan was materialising well until he remembered the last of the cardinal rules, which was to depart the bank quickly. He expected to be so laden with money that a getaway on foot was unrealistic. He had to have a getaway car. That's when Fat Ron came into the picture. Mind you, he was so fat, he took up the whole picture. Anyway, Rod turned to Fat Ron to be his getaway driver. Neither of them had a car, but that was no problem, as Fat Ron would steal a car a few hours before the robbery. It was agreed that Fat Ron would receive 20% of the take for his part in getting Rod away quickly from the scene of the crime, as time was of essence. Rod's plan was supposed to be fool proof. Rod told Fat Ron that he wanted to rob the bank near his place the following day at 3:30pm and he told him to find a car for a pickup at 3:10pm, which would give him 20 minutes to get to the bank. Fat Ron, for his 20% share, would source a car, take him there and wait at the bank ready for the getaway.

The next day at 3:10, Rod was all dressed up, excited

and shaking slightly with adrenaline. He had secreted the shotgun in a large duffel bag, which for the time being was empty but would soon be full of money. Peering through the front curtains of his parole house, Rod couldn't believe his eyes when he saw what was in the driveway. Fat Ron sat there in the smallest car possible, a beaten-up old Toyota Corolla hatchback that Fat Ron had somehow squeezed into. It only had two doors and a yellowy-orange duco that could only be described as the colour of baby poo. It was extremely conspicuous and utterly recognisable.

Reluctantly, Rod ran out to the car. Firstly, he had trouble opening the door with his gloved hand, secondly, he had trouble fitting into the passenger seat with his bulky helmet, and thirdly, he struggled to accommodate the duffel bag that rested on his lap. As he squeezed into the car, he looked across to his fat mate and exclaimed, "What the fuck is this heap of shit?" Fat Ron wasn't sure if Rod was referring to the small size, the age, condition or colour of the car – or all of the above – and replied defensively, "It was the only one without an alarm that was unlocked."

It was a manual car and Fat Ron had difficulty changing gears as they made their way to the bank. Before they reached it, they had to drive through a school zone and had to slow down to a mere 40km/h. Fat Ron made a mental note to not drive through the school zone when making their getaway. An alternative route would be far more desirable if they were going to get away quickly, or even at all. It wasn't long before Fat Ron parked the Corolla in a loading zone in front of the bank. He kept the engine running as Rod clambered out of the Corolla with great difficulty. He finally got out, adjusted his helmet and unzipped the duffel bag in readiness. It only took him six strides to enter the bank. As he did so, he produced the shotgun and screamed at the top of his lungs, "This is a robbery! Don't fucken move or you're dead."

He quickly moved towards the stunned tellers, pushing the only customer aside with the shotgun. Rod was in full control and systematically went to each of the tellers demanding they put cash into the open duffel bag. Just like in his mental rehearsals, everything was going to plan. The customer did not interfere, and he methodically collected over $5,000 in cash, for just a few minutes of work. All eyes were on the shotgun that he waved around; no one was prepared to find out if it was loaded or not.

After the last teller's transfer of cash, he shouted, "Don't follow me, or else!" and quickly exited the bank. The customer and tellers had no intention of following him and were more than prepared to obey his commands, however, they couldn't help but see the robber leaving the bank, clearly see him, in fact, through the bank's glass façade. They saw him throw the duffel bag into the open passenger door; they saw him squeeze himself into the tiny baby-poo coloured car; they watched as it sped off down the street. In fact, one of the tellers even knew it to be a Corolla as he had the same model of car, albeit in a far nicer colour.

Rod barely got his legs, helmet and the shotgun, now separated from its bag, into the car as Fat Ron took off. He drove at break-neck speed around the block, avoiding the school traffic zone, and made his way directly to Rod's place. He parked the car in the driveway and they both got out, each with his own difficulty. When inside they were elated with their achievement and gave each other high fives and hugs. Fat Ron was hard to hug because of his immense girth but Rod managed to, as nothing would stand in the way of his joy.

Rod poured the cash over the coffee table and stood back in admiration. After a few moments he composed himself sufficiently to start counting the takings. Fat Ron wasn't allowed to count it, he just watched and waited for his share. After some checking and double-checking, the total was agreed to be $6,420. Fat Ron reminded Rod that his share was 20% – whatever that came to. He had no idea how much he was going to get, but he trusted his co-conspirator to be honest with him. Rod counted out $1,000 and handed it to Fat Ron telling him that that was 20%, and as a bonus, he could keep the car. Fat Ron was moved by Rod's generosity and left after giving Rod another grateful hug.

The police had little trouble locating the Corolla. It had been reported stolen that morning, so the registration was known to them, and they also had a clear description given by the bank staff. As a result, Fat Ron was stopped by police while he was driving the car some few kilometres away from Rod's place. When the police asked him about the car, the cash and the bank robbery, he squealed like a pig, implicating Rod immediately and exposing the supposedly fool-proof plan.

In the meantime, Rod separated out the $200 cash that he owed for the shotgun and placed the balance of the cash into the duffel bag with the shotgun, helmet and gloves. He had a very good night's sleep only to be woken by police early the next morning at 4am. They were armed and wore body armour, and kicked the door down before presenting their search warrant. Rod was told his legal rights – that he didn't have to answer their questions and that any answers he gave could be used against him in court. Rod was arrested at first on suspicion, but when police found the duffel bag and its incriminating contents, he was charged with the armed bank robbery. Rod floundered, as arrest had not been part of the plan he had rehearsed. At the end of the judicial process, Fat Ron received a lean sentence of two years as an accessory and Rod received a fat sentence of eight years for being a bank bandit.

With the passage of time, banks have implemented better security measures and the armed bank robber has become a rare species. You might think that all those idle sawn-off shotguns were doomed to extinction. Not so. The advent of the modern drug culture has restored the sawn-off shotgun's significance and usefulness.

No better example is to be found, than the 2017 home invasion of a supposed drug house in Cooloongup, a new working-class residential area on the outskirts of Perth. I represented one of the three masked and armed raiders who had invaded the home looking for drugs and cash. A common misconception amongst criminals is that one can rob a drug house with relative impunity as its occupants are unlikely to report the incident to the police because of their own criminal activity. This rationale is somewhat misguided, however, when their criminality and actions are far more serious than those of the drug dealer.

When these three raiders stormed this suburban home, they thought there would be large stashes of drugs and money. They had been tipped off by associates and decided that it was worth exploiting, as they did not expect that police would get involved. As it approached midnight, they armed themselves with a sawn-off shotgun, a baseball bat and a tomahawk axe and made their way to the tranquil residence. The three were high on meth and when they got there, they rushed from the car and barged their way into the home in single file. The leader of the gang, armed with the sawn-off shotgun, went first as he felt the most empowered, followed closely by the axeman and then the baseballer. As soon he arrived inside the darkened home, he fired the shotgun broadside across the lounge room. Whether this shot was a wakeup call, a warning shot or had lethal intent, is impossible to know, but what he soon discovered was that there were three children sleeping in the lounge room.

It wasn't long before the terrified father confronted the gang. They demanded all his "gear" and "cash", while pointing the shotgun at him. The house was no longer dark as the father had switched the lights on in his panic as the dazed and crying children appeared amongst the gunpowder haze. The sordid scene, however, did not weaken the raiders' resolve, as they kept demanding drugs and cash. The father denied that he had either drugs or cash and ordered that they leave the house. It was then the gang leader shouted, "Give us a pound of gear or I'll take a pound of flesh!" This demand was meaningless to the father as he again pleaded that he had neither drugs nor cash. The ringleader then fired the shotgun a second time, this time at point blank range right through the father's left leg, causing a horrific injury and splintering bone and flesh. The three raiders burst outside and left in a hurry as the father screamed in pain. The tibia of his left leg had multiple fractures and the main blood vessel below the knee had been severed. This caused the leg to die and it eventually needed to be amputated.

When the raiders were sentenced as a trio, the Supreme Court judge described the attack and home invasion as a "horrifying, traumatic ordeal for all the victims [...] in particular for the children", and went on to say that "it does not take a great deal of imagination to think of the lasting psychological harm such offending would cause the children."

As defence counsel, neither I, nor the other two legal representatives had much to say in mitigation. Unfortunately, my client, who was thirty-eight years old at the time, had an extensive criminal record and little could be said on his behalf or in his favour. His Honour regarded the offending at the highest level of criminality and imposed a total of 28 years imprisonment combined for the trio. The specific sentences were 12 years imprisonment for the shot gunner, eight years for my client, the axeman, and eight years for the base baller. This brazen raid did little more than expose three villains and demonstrate the enduring appeal of the sawn-off shotgun to outlaws, bandits, robbers and drug enforcers.

# Meth Heads

Brandon was a troubled nineteen-year-old Aboriginal man, who before this incident had previously just smoked a little pot with his friends. When he was just a baby, his father died and his mother had abandoned him. He was brought up by his uncle and aunt in a dysfunctional and chaotic household that was marred by neglect, as well as alcohol and drug abuse. Pot smoking affects some people more than others, and can compound issues connected to unresolved trauma. Unfortunately for Brandon, he had been diagnosed at seventeen with paranoid psychosis and schizophrenia.

Fast forward two years and Brandon was sharing a rental home with five others, one of whom was his girlfriend. They lived in the town of Hedland, located in the rich iron ore region of the Pilbara, in north-west Australia. At the time of this incident he was out of work and couldn't really afford drugs.

On this fateful day, his best friend Jake brought over some methamphetamine to the house and offered it to Brandon and his girlfriend. It was mid-afternoon when Jake injected the ice in front of the others as Brandon cut up a cannabis bud with some scissors before smoking it. They were aimlessly passing time and seemed to enjoy hanging out and getting wasted together. For whatever reason, be it sheer boredom or the quest for some excitement, Brandon decided to join in, and experienced the rush of meth for the first time. It didn't take long, however, before the effect of the ice created tension between the two friends. Brandon took exception to the way Jake was looking at his girlfriend's legs and made it known to him, exclaiming, "Fuck off, stop perving! She's my girl."

Jake was still holding the needle he had just used and seemed pre-occupied indeed with Brandon's girlfriend's legs. Brandon, in the meantime, was sitting on the lounge next to his girlfriend, across from Jake. It took Jake a few moments for the reprimand to register. When it did, he jumped up suddenly and took a step towards Brandon. It was an aggressive move and Brandon felt intimidated. So he also jumped up and started to move backwards, away from Jake, towards the front door. By this time, Jake was shaping up to Brandon with the needle still in his hand.

Not only did Jake look extremely threatening, he also punched Brandon in the face. Brandon responded by grabbing the pair of scissors that were now lying passively on the entry sideboard, and instinctively stabbed his best friend once in the chest. The scissors cut through Jake's flimsy t-shirt and into his body, penetrating his lung and aorta. The blow caused him to drop to the floor where he lay motionless with blood pouring from the wound. As Jake lay bleeding to death on the floor, Brandon exited through the front door. On his way out, he smashed up a timber chair in the front yard and took one of its legs to use as a weapon, should it be necessary. He then decided to go back into the house to get his girlfriend, however when he saw Jake on the floor, unresponsive, he realised the gravity of the situation and promptly fled the house. His girlfriend shakily called an ambulance.

For two days, Brandon hid in a drainpipe on the outskirts of town while a police manhunt ensued. During this time he came down from the drugs and was forced to confront what he had done. He decided to give himself up and so surrendered to the police, who had otherwise made little progress with the extensive manhunt.

Brandon was charged with murder, which in the Criminal Code is defined as an unlawful killing when there is an intention to cause the death or cause bodily harm of such a nature as to endanger life. The code also states that alternatively, murder is committed if the death is caused by an act done in the prosecution of an unlawful purpose, which is likely to endanger human life.

Subsequently, at Brandon's murder trial, I was his counsel and raised the motive of self-defence to explain his action. To establish self-defence, Brandon had to satisfy the Court that he believed the stabbing of his best friend was necessary for him to defend himself and was, in the circumstances, a reasonable response.

The presiding female judge with her flowing robes, make up and coiffure, looked resplendent during Brandon's jury trial. The prosecutor forewarned me that he intended to tender into evidence some graphic photos of the deceased's chest showing the wound with the scissors sticking out of it. The photos weren't simply graphic, they were distressing and repulsive. I applied to the judge, in the absence of the jury, and requested that these photos not be shown to the jury as they were likely to cause them no small degree of anguish. I further argued that the photos had no probative value and weren't necessary in the prosecution of the case, as the prosecutor could rely on a volume of other evidence. I said that the facts and circumstances of death were not in issue, having been admitted on the basis that the defence was one of self-defence. I stressed that it was unnecessary to traumatise the jury with these photos and said that they could unfairly evoke a malevolent prejudice towards the accused.

Her Honour was dismissive of my submission, making me feel like a dinosaur and out of touch with modernity. Obviously, she was a new breed of judge, and well familiar with modern-day customs, unlike me, the aging defence counsel standing before her. She retorted that she had full confidence that in this day of reality crime TV and gory films the jurors would not find such photos distressing.

She therefore ruled that they could be shown to the jury.

Upon Her Honour's ruling, the jury returned to the courtroom for the continuation of the trial. The prosecutor, with aplomb, handed the photos to the jury foreperson who took one look at them and promptly fainted. The Court went into overdrive as Her Honour announced an urgent adjournment. Jurors and security guards rushed to assist the foreperson while someone hurried in search of medical help. The adjournment continued for another half hour before the foreperson gained sufficient composure to resume the trial. Of course, the photos continued to be distributed amongst the jurors who had now braced themselves for the gory experience and no one else fainted.

Later, however, my client nearly fainted with relief when the jury acquitted him of murder. They must have accepted that Brandon's stabbing of Jake was a reasonable and necessary act in the circumstances of Jake's intimidation and assault. Brandon was convicted of the lesser charge of manslaughter. Manslaughter, in this case, was the unlawful killing of Jake without Brandon having had the intention to cause the death or bodily harm to endanger Jake's life. That is, he was justified in defending himself, but his actions were excessive in the circumstances. Brandon received a moderate term of six years imprisonment, with the possibility of release on parole after serving only four years.

This result angered the victim's family who were not appeased by white man's justice and instigated a demand that Brandon, upon his release, be punished under Aboriginal tribal law. Brandon heard this news on the prison grapevine and was resolved to accept whatever tribal punishment he was going to receive, probably a form of payback by spearing. Aboriginal tribal law of payback is still practised to this day. Traditional law, which has a history of over 40,000 years, runs parallel to the Australian legal system and is sometimes in conflict with it, due to the perceived violence of some of its practices. Payback, performed by the aggrieved victim, or their family or tribe, is often administered by spearing or "singing". The punishment of spearing is exactly what it sounds like and the spear is usually aimed at the offender's thigh. The punishment of "singing" is a curse, sometimes referred to as "pointing the bone", that is called down by a senior elder of the tribe to cause harm to the offender. Only time will tell if Brandon will be cursed or speared, or both.

It is most unfortunate that methamphetamine ruined two lives that day. Jake was dead at the hand of his best friend, and Brandon would never be the same again, having killed him.

# An Eye for an Eye

The evening news was on the television in the common room of the remand wing of Hakea Prison, in an outer suburb of Perth. The wing housed the cells of prisoners awaiting their trials or who had pending court appearances. A small group of prisoners were watching the news, including my client Tom. He was waiting for his day in court on charges of burglary.

Coincidentally, the news announcer said that police were investigating a serious assault upon a young girl that had occurred some days earlier, and it so happened that this girl was Tom's niece, whom he was very fond of. As the announcer continued with the unfortunate story, the face of the suspect filled the TV screen. It made for an extremely awkward situation, as Tom instantly recognised the face as belonging to the guy sitting next to him. The prison authorities weren't aware of the connection between Tom, his niece, the suspect and the story, and neither, for that matter, was his fellow inmate. It was pure coincidence that both were on remand in the same section of the prison, for completely different reasons. Tom was there for charges of burglary and the other was there for allegedly sexually assaulting the niece.

Due to the brutish nature of prison life, many prisoners arm themselves for protection. Tom often carried a sharpened pencil – not intended for writing, but for stabbing. A pencil to most people is nothing more than a somewhat outdated and innocuous writing instrument, but for Tom it was a potent weapon. Fortuitously for him, though not for his intended victim, Tom was in possession of his sharpened pencil and he intended to use it as a weapon of revenge upon his new-found enemy. He surreptitiously wrapped his fist around the pencil, allowing it to protrude a few centimetres from his calloused fingers. Without a second thought, in a single motion he thrust the makeshift dagger into the suspect's neck. The suspect, now the victim, was seated on Tom's left and did not see the attack coming. Neither had he expected any trouble. He had been simply watching the news, and unfortunately for him, he had become the news.

The pencil entered the right side of his neck and pierced the external jugular vein. Blood went everywhere, and the other viewers scattered. Mayhem broke out as other prisoners took the chaotic situation as an opportunity to attack their own enemies. In a short time, many grievances and disputes were settled, resulting in several broken bones and many bruised knuckles. It took the guards some time to settle things and get to the victim who now lay unconscious on the floor, bleeding profusely. His jugular vein was ruptured and was spewing blood. The victim was unresponsive, while a commercial on the TV expounded the joys of buying an "Oh what a feeling" Toyota.

Meanwhile, the bloodied pencil was still in my client's hand when he was subdued and dragged out of the room by fellow inmates. Despite the great number of witnesses, not one was prepared to give evidence against Tom; the code of silence was deafening and adhered to by all, in the interests of self-preservation.

To dob on a fellow inmate is a very dangerous course of action that is viewed in prison logic as an unforgivable act of betrayal. Inmates regard informants as "rats" and "dogs" and punish them at any opportunity for their supposed treachery. For this reason, it is unusual for a prisoner to "rat" on a fellow inmate for the obvious reasons of retaliation. But sometimes the crime is so serious that inmates who are key witnesses are offered police protection to induce them to give evidence.

In this case, the injury and its consequences could have been far more serious but for the fact that medical assistance came quickly. A prison guard used his bare hands to stanch the gushing blood and apply pressure to the victim's neck until a proper bandage could be applied.

Unfortunately for Tom, the common room was sufficiently lit for the ceiling-mounted camera to capture the whole incident. Tom was first charged with attempted murder but later that charge was downgraded to unlawful wounding. The camera footage showed Tom sitting next to the victim and without any warning or hint of any aggressive body language, Tom appeared to punch the victim in the right side of the neck. As one looked closer, however, it was clear that the punch was not a punch, but a swinging thrust with the bottom of his fist. Though no weapon was visible, the nature of the wound stated the obvious – that a sharp object must have been used. Having the identity of the assailant clearly depicted on the footage, it was now a matter of searching Tom and his cell for the weapon.

The search delivered two apparent weapons, and both were pencils. Tom was no Shakespeare and wasn't writing a manuscript, so the pencils looked suspicious. One was sharp, and had blood on it and the other was blunt and smeared with faeces. Obviously, only one of the pencils was used as evidence for this charge. Even though the eyewitness inmates refused to say anything incriminating against Tom, the camera evidence was overwhelming. He pleaded guilty so there was no need for a trial. Because of this plea, the victim did not have to give evidence against my client, which was a great relief for both of them. Tom received a sentence of two years imprisonment without eligibility for parole, so he had to serve his full term.

With the passage of time, the victim's neck fully healed

and his own court case rolled around. He defended the serious charge of sexual assault upon Tom's niece. Tom followed the case with intense interest and was elated when he heard that his victim, now a defendant, had been convicted of that charge and was to be sentenced. Tom was looking forward to their reunion.

On another occasion of coincidence and misfortune, another client of mine called Rick was sitting on a barstool drinking beer at a seedy pub on the outskirts of Perth. The barstools stood high and had solid wooden backrests, which allowed the patrons to lean backwards and relax at the bar whilst enjoying a beer or two. It so happened that Rick was happily partaking of a few cold beers and minding his own business while watching the television that was mounted above the bar. He had ridden his motorcycle to this pub and although he usually rode with a gang of patched associates, on this occasion he was a lone wolf.

As always, he carried a large knife sheathed inside the top of his left boot. While he was on his fourth beer, a stranger came in and sat on the barstool next to him, to his immediate right. He heard the stool move but was not interested in making the stranger's acquaintance. He was fixated on the television, which was featuring his late mother. At thirty-four years of age she had been a prominent brothel owner in Western Australia and had been mysteriously murdered several years before. The crime had not been solved nor had the killer been found. She had been in the prostitution business for a long time and had a history of witchcraft and black magic. Her body had been found at dawn, slumped behind the wheel of her Dodge Phoenix sedan parked near the Royal Perth golf course. She was dressed in a formal gown, wearing expensive jewellery and had four bullet holes in her head.

While the stranger was getting comfortable on his wooden barstool and before he ordered a beer, he glanced at the TV, and noticing the subject of the program, exclaimed, "She got what she deserved." Rick did not need an invitation. He spontaneously reached down to his left boot, grabbed the knife with his right hand and swung it half orbit, piercing the chest of the stranger and pinning him to the back of the stool. The knife penetrated the stranger's heart and firmly stuck into the wooden back of the stool, killing him instantly. He was unlucky to have made an invidious comment to the son of this infamous madam. Rick found the stranger's comment insulting in the extreme, and so provoking that he impulsively and violently reacted.

Violence had always been a large part of Rick's world, and it didn't take much for him to lose control. He had unresolved anger issues, evidenced in a long criminal record that boasted many crimes of violence, ranging from assaults to grievous bodily harm. Rick was convicted of wilful murder for this brutal stabbing and was sentenced to life imprisonment with a minimum of 16 years to serve before parole. In the circumstances, the ruling was not excessive and sat at the lower end of the sentencing scale. I was involved in the appeal against Rick's conviction, which was unfortunately unsuccessful, although the outcome was not as unfortunate as that received by the deceased stranger.

Parole is the drawbridge between stymied prison regimentation and the freedom of civic liberty. It provides the criminal with the opportunity to prove his or her own standing by transitioning them from a lifestyle of crime and punishment to that of a law-abiding citizen. A judge at sentencing usually stipulates eligibility for parole when imposing a term of imprisonment, and this means that the term of imprisonment stays the same and only the period of custody is reduced. In other words, a sentence of, say, six years imprisonment with eligibility for parole would require the prisoner to serve at least four years in custody and two years on parole.

During parole, the prisoner serves out his or her sentence in the community with imposed terms and conditions, of which the cardinal condition is "not reoffending". That doesn't mean they are allowed to offend *after* the parole period – but so many do. This doesn't necessarily mean that society or the parole board have failed them, as many do-gooders claim; the fact is they have failed themselves. In some instances, when a prisoner has previously breached parole, or has such a bad criminal record that there is a real risk of reoffending, parole is denied. This means the full sentence has to be served in custody.

Despite the fact that a sentencing judge orders a prisoner's eligibility for parole, the granting of parole does not automatically occur, as it is up to the parole board to decide the question of eligibility. If a prisoner breaks the law and/or prison rules during their sentence, the quest for parole eligibility is regressed and sometimes shattered, requiring them to serve their full sentence. "Recidivists" are habitual or career criminals who generally are denied parole because society is no longer prepared to accommodate or tolerate the likelihood of their reoffending. In the eyes of society, they are deemed to be something of a "lost cause". Jail is as much a reality for the recidivist as tax is to the average hard-working Australian. Neither is keen for it, but that's the cost of law and order.

# The Australia Day Murder

Ask yourself this: how could it be that a twenty-six-year-old Aboriginal man was stabbed to death with a screwdriver at a busy Perth train station by eight strangers? It is a fair question that may be asked by any law-abiding citizen.

On the evening of Australia Day in 2016, the fireworks display over the Perth foreshore was mesmerising for the thousands of citizens who lined the banks of the Swan River. However, two groups of Indigenous trouble makers were totally uninterested in that spectacle and were more keen on the fireworks they themselves could cause as they wandered through the streets of Perth.

Like strutting peacocks, the males were showing off to the few females in the group. Despite the fact that most of them were unemployed, they were all wearing the latest brand name clothing. They walked the streets as if they owned them and road rules didn't apply. They felt invincible, fuelled by various illicit substances and their delinquent attitude. The streets were theirs even though they never paid a cent in tax towards their upkeep, nor were they likely to in the future. After the fireworks, the residents of Perth returned home with their families. All that was left behind on the Swan River foreshore was refuse and these marauders.

My client, Trent, was twenty-nine, and the only non-Indigenous person amongst this lot. He was of medium height with pasty white skin and mousy hair. It so happened that during the fireworks show earlier that evening, he had been locked up by police for prior disorderly conduct. His left hand was bandaged because he had dislocated it punching a reinforced window advertisement at a bus stop. Trent was not sharing in the spirit of the Australia Day celebrations, other than in his consumption of alcohol.

That night, Trent had no agenda and no expectations. He was moping around on his own with aimless intent, happy to see what fate had in store for him. Maybe he would find some adventure. Along the way he hoped to score some drugs and join up with others of a similar mindset. After leaving the Perth train station he shadowed a group of youths for a while and then, nonchalantly, joined them. This group of young people comprised at least eight males, aged between eleven and twenty-six years, and a few females in their late teens. Trent didn't know anyone in the group but as they didn't tell him to "fuck off," he tagged along.

It was a fateful decision that he made, because before long, this group, including Trent, got into a violent fight with another group of Indigenous youths. It was now 3am and the street CCTV captured the young women from each group bitterly fighting, pulling each other's hair and wrestling, whilst the men watched and threw bottles at each other. The fighting escalated and one male magically produced a hammer, which he used to strike the back of the head of a young man from Trent's group. Another ripped his shirt off and showed with pride his dark skin, glistening in the streetlights. This half-naked male was seen running around punching and gouging others, including some of the fighting females. Trent, by his mere presence, was now an inductee into this group as they moved away from the other combatants and the mayhem.

However, it wasn't long before these two groups again crossed paths and the rolling battle resumed. Other CCTV footage captured individuals arming themselves with sticks, rocks and objects stolen from a nearby construction site. They used these objects as weapons against each other. All of a sudden, a white Holden Commodore station wagon pulled up and its driver, apparently a mate of Trent's group, jumped out of the vehicle and went around the back to open the rear tailgate. As if it had been previously rehearsed, some of Trent's group ran towards the open tailgate and collected more sticks and other weapons from the car. The CCTV footage showed them giving chase to the other group, who had now retreated towards the escalators at the Esplanade train station. The eventual victim was amongst the group that took flight up the escalators, followed closely by Trent and his mob in hot pursuit.

There is vision of my client carrying and then throwing two glass bottles. Others of his group are seen carrying an iron star picket, a long dark pole, rocks, bottles and a slender silver object. The victim is last seen alive at 3:07am on the CCTV, running away from Trent's mob. His final moments were spent running from the eight armed assailants. Unfortunately for him, he was the largest and slowest of his group and fell behind, allowing Trent's group to catch up and prey upon him. The actual attack was not captured on CCTV because it occurred in a dark alcove and out of view of the camera, however forensic evidence of the footage sequence suggested that the fatal attack lasted only fifty seconds. Following that, Trent and the others can be seen leaving the scene and returning gingerly to the top of the escalator. It also appears that one of them is holding a screwdriver and others the iron star picket and pole. The bottles and rocks had been dispatched in the attack and were no longer in Trent's nor anyone in the group's possession.

After Trent and his cohort rode back down the escalator, which had previously delivered them to the victim, they scattered in all directions, out of sight of the CCTV cameras. The victim was found lying supine and unresponsive, outside the closed entrance of a coffee shop on the concourse of the first level. Paramedics arrived at 3:43am and could not detect any breathing or pulse. The victim was in cardiac arrest and CPR was administered. Paramedics noticed a puncture wound to the upper left side of his chest and numerous other wounds to his body and head. The paramedics continued treatment in the ambulance as they transported him as a priority one patient to Royal Perth Hospital. Soon after arrival at 4:31am the victim was pronounced deceased.

The post-mortem examination revealed no fewer than twenty-three external injuries, including the fatal stab wound. It was determined that the cause of death was a single penetrating injury to the left side of the front of the chest, which penetrated the victim's aorta and lungs. The approximate length of the fatal wound track was 2.55cm, with the direction of the wound track being from left to right, downwards and backwards. In the investigation, police located a large screwdriver, which had been discarded on a nearby construction site. Evidence at trial confirmed that this screwdriver was the likely weapon that caused the fatal injury, even though each of the eight accused denied delivering the blow that killed the victim.

After Trent fled the scene, he saw the incident reported on the TV news the following evening, and it was then that he realised the victim was dead. He panicked and burnt the clothes he had been wearing that night. He also attempted to change his appearance by shaving off his scruffy beard.

With the CCTV footage, fingerprints and DNA results, the suspects were rounded up very quickly. No longer were they peacocks with ostentatious plumage, they were more like chickens about to be plucked. Trent, the other six adult males and one eleven-year-old boy, were charged with murder. Each pleaded not guilty and went to trial before a judge and jury in the Supreme Court of Western Australia. During the six-week trial, my client admitted he was "fucked up that night" with alcohol and heroin. He said he had thrown a couple of bottles that had missed the target and had only kicked the victim in the back and head a few times. He had to use his foot to kick with, as his hand was bandaged and sore. His only intention in attacking the victim had been to "make him piss" – that is, to kick him and jump on him to hurt but not kill him.

Not only did Trent not know the people in the group he was with, he didn't know the others in the victim's group either. He had just gone with the flow. He was prepared to get involved in a rolling brawl with strangers against strangers. He didn't think that anyone would get killed. He described himself to police as a "sheep" and "a follower" who readily gave into peer pressure and just went along for the thrill of it.

In contradiction to Trent's story, the CCTV footage played in the courtroom didn't depict him as a sheep or follower, but more as a leader in the attack, running up the escalator, hurling bottles and baying for blood. Despite his attempts to play down his involvement, the police gathered evidence for a strong prosecution case. The state's case was compelling against Trent and his group. The state alleged that each of the eight had acted together in murdering the deceased. Even though their roles were different, they acted in concert, and collectively precipitated the death of a total stranger.

In the sixth week of the trial, the jury unanimously convicted each accused, including my client Trent, of murder. At the jury verdict of the trial, there was additional security present at the Supreme Court. Guards banned some of the accused's family members from returning, after they had acted inappropriately, shouting out obscenities and threats during the trial proceedings. There had also been a sidewalk altercation outside the Court between family members of the convicted prisoners and the mother of the deceased. The grieving mother was mocked with the despicable words of "at least our boys ain't dead!"

Trent received a life sentence, with a minimum of 18 years to serve before parole. The others also received sentences of life imprisonment with minimums of between 16 and 18 years. Another received 12 months minimum because he had been a juvenile at the time of the offence. The sixteen-year-old boy pleaded guilty to the lesser charge of manslaughter, after entering into a plea bargain with the prosecution during the third day of trial. He was sentenced to four-and-a-half years of juvenile detention. The eleven-year-old child, the youngest of the group, was separately tried in the Children's Court and his identity was protected by a public suppression order.

This story is a cautionary tale for those who succumb to peer group pressure and follow the herd, as in this case, *birds of a feather do life in prison together.*

# The "Innocent" Drug Smuggler

I n 2014, I represented Cody, an American tourist in his mid-fifties. He had arrived at the Perth International Airport for the first time in his life, having travelled from Texas via Manila, the capital of the Philippines, where he had a pre-arranged stopover. He was carrying two large suitcases, a small carry-on bag and three mobile phones. Upon his arrival in Perth, he was processed through passport control and customs. One of the diligent customs officers became suspicious of Cody after discovering that one of his suitcases contained women's clothing and toiletries. As Cody was travelling alone and clearly was a male, this oddity alerted the officer who proceeded to conduct a thorough search. In the lining of that suitcase, the officer and his colleagues found a large quantity of white powder, which turned out to be three kilograms of methamphetamine with an average purity of 78.6% and a potential street value of upwards of $4 million. There was nothing illegal found in the other suitcase or the carry bag, though the fact that Cody carried three mobile phones was also deemed suspicious.

Cody instantly went from tourist to suspect as he was arrested and charged with importing a commercial quantity of a border-controlled drug. His protestations that it wasn't his and that he knew nothing about it fell on deaf ears. He was remanded in custody until his trial, which was given some priority and was heard a mere nine months later in the District Court of Western Australia before a judge and jury.

The jury process involves the selection of at least twelve jurors for a trial from a panel of people randomly produced from the electoral role who are required to attend court on the first day of trial. The defence counsel and prosecutor are given a list of the prospective jurors, represented by a number that codifies their full name, address and occupation. This succinct information gives a snapshot of the juror's background that may be relevant for jury selection. Usually more than twelve jurors are selected for long trials, being a form of insurance against sickness, and a ballot is drawn at the end of the evidence for the required twelve jurors.

In the selection process, defence counsel can challenge up to three prospective jurors by way of announcing a peremptory challenge before that juror takes the oath or affirmation. On the other hand, the prosecution can also challenge up to three prospective jurors for each accused standing trial. No reason needs to be given and each juror's confidentiality is maintained by referring to that juror by their given number. This system of qualified anonymity provides a safeguard to ensure that the jury is representative of the community. These challenges by defence counsel and the prosecutor expediently remove prospective jurors that they know or believe may not be impartial for whatever reason.

As Cody's counsel at trial, and pursuant to his instructions, I led the defence of "lack of knowledge" – namely that Cody had no knowledge of the drugs that were concealed in the suitcase he carried. His evidence on oath was that he had been tricked into smuggling the drugs by a British lawyer, a Mr Rowland Booth. He said that some time before his travels, while he was still residing in Texas, he received an unsolicited email from Mr Booth, who identified himself as a lawyer and advised Cody that he was the lucky recipient of an inheritance of no less than £10.5 million British pounds. To collect his entitlement, Mr Booth convinced Cody to travel, as directed by him, in order to execute the necessary documents that would enable him to collect the inheritance. Apparently his ticket to Perth, via Manila, had been purchased and paid for by Mr Booth, for this purpose. This travel itinerary might have been considered suspicious in its own right, however Cody had obediently followed the instructions, as he was elated to be travelling at someone else's expense with the prospect of collecting a substantial fortune.

Cody travelled alone and with great expectation. He was instructed by Mr Booth that on his way to Perth his flight would take him through the Philippines with a stopover in Manila. There he would meet a woman whose name was Jacinta, who was a friend of Mr Booth's. She was very pleasant when she met Cody at the airport, and after a few days of showing him the sights of Manila, she asked him for a favour. Because she knew Mr Booth, and because the meeting with her had been pre-arranged by him, Cody was happy to oblige. Jacinta asked him to take a suitcase with him to Perth containing clothes and toiletries she was sending to a female relative who resided there. To make it worth his time, she told him she had arranged with this relative to pay Cody $1,000 cash for his troubles, which he would receive upon arrival. Despite having his own suitcase, he agreed to the request to help Jacinta out, as well as to enjoy the extra $1,000 of spending money for his time in Perth. He obviously gave little thought to the fact that the value of the clothing and toiletries was unlikely to be more than the $1,000 he was to receive as reward for his services.

Later in court, he said that when he got Jacinta's suitcase, he did open it in her presence and browsed through the various items that appeared consistent with her description. The contents looked innocuous and harmless and he later said that his suspicions had not been aroused by Jacinta or the suitcase, even though the request was unusual. He was prepared to do her the favour, was happy to receive the $1,000, and hoped that it would also reflect well on him in the eyes of Mr Booth. Cody told the authorities that he left Manila without knowing the true contents of Jacinta's suitcase or the true intentions of her or Mr Booth.

After he gave his evidence, the prosecutor cross-examined him, challenging his honesty and truthfulness. The prosecutor asserted that his explanation was untrue and concocted. Further, it was put to Cody that no one would have entrusted such a valuable quantity of drugs to a courier, without letting them know their value, and the obligation to deliver them where required. This was serious business and the consequences could be dire.

I argued on Cody's behalf that he had been groomed by Mr Booth and tricked into smuggling the drugs into Perth without actual knowledge of the drugs themselves. I further submitted that in his evidence, it was apparent that while Cody may have had some suspicions of being scammed by Mr Booth, he was, in any event, naively prepared to go along with the proposal, as he enjoyed travel and was otherwise unable to afford it. In addition, he was still hopeful of getting his windfall inheritance even though it may have only been wishful thinking.

The Jury, after some considerable deliberation, returned a verdict of not guilty and acquitted Cody who responded with a great sigh of relief. Cody clearly was an unsuspecting and "innocent" drug smuggler. He made urgent travel arrangements at his own expense this time, boarded the next available flight to America and has not been seen or heard of since.

# The Vietnam Veteran

Nick was a first generation Aussie. His parents immigrated to Australia in 1949, having been displaced from Eastern Europe after the Second World War. When they arrived in Australia they had just married and had no more than ten pounds in their pockets. They were both in their early twenties, had one suitcase between them and neither could speak any English. The English language was extremely difficult for them to understand and near impossible to learn.

They had free passage to Australia and their destination was Melbourne. However, the ship broke down in the port of Fremantle so they disembarked and arbitrarily decided to make Perth their home instead. They could have gone to Canada or the USA, as many of their friends had chosen to do, but they were induced to venture to

Australia where they were told employment was guaranteed, and opportunities abounded. They did not foresee the prejudice they would suffer, and 18 years later, the sacrifice they would be forced to make for their new and adopted country.

In due course, they would farewell their teenage son Nick to serve in the Vietnam War by way of compulsory National Service. After fleeing their own war-torn country and being uprooted from their culture and customs, it became evident that their newfound democracy would come at a terrible price. Previously, the enemy had stolen their home, land and culture. Now a new enemy had emerged in Vietnam, ready to further impact their family.

Nick's mother worked in a tuna cannery and cycled to work each day while his father worked as a machinist in an asbestos factory. Their dreams of attaining the professions or careers that would have been achievable in their old country evaporated when they landed on Australian soil as penniless migrants. They were nevertheless forever grateful for their new freedom and status as citizens of a democracy. Nick, their only child, was sheltered by his parents to the extent that when he started school at five years of age, he couldn't speak or understand any English. Along with his parents, Nick was cocooned in a home that bore witness to the old world, the old country, and his parent's previous life, customs and language.

As time passed, Nick had the love and support he needed to be a good son and student. His parents' hard work in menial jobs allowed them to send him to a private Christian school and it gave him the best education that they could afford. They hoped he would attain a professional life and the prosperity that had alluded them.

When Nick was drafted by birthday ballot into the National Service he went enthusiastically, as he knew no better at eighteen years of age than to obediently serve his country. Anyway, it was only for two years – what could possibly go wrong? He had qualified to go to university to study engineering, but that plan had to wait until he returned from his stint in the Army. In Vietnam, Nick's secondment was the Australian Signals and Communications Corps and soon after arriving in Vietnam he experienced frontline action at Lon Tan. One night he and his squad were on a reconnaissance patrol and did not anticipate contact with the enemy. During a short break, Nick and his best buddy were sitting on a log, when an enemy sniper shot his mate through the head. The shock and trauma of what he witnessed that night caused Nick post-traumatic stress and long-term neurosis.

He survived the war, but returned a very different young man, harbouring that tragedy and still grieving for his mate. The public hostility towards the Vietnam War and criticism of its veterans did not help his condition, indeed probably aggravated it. His parents hoped that upon his return, he would begin his studies at university, as this would give him a profession as an engineer and bring kudos to the modest family.

Nick tried to please his parents, but his mental condition prevented any return to normality, and he started using cannabis together with prescribed medication. Much to his parents' disappointment, he abandoned any thought of studying at university. He tried but couldn't find employment, nor was he too fussed to do so, as his focus settled on drugs and the relief they brought him. He was also starting to suffer intermittent depression, which further reinforced his need for drugs as a chemical solution. It didn't take long for him to develop a serious drug addiction and he graduated to hard drugs such as cocaine and heroin.

In a story that is all too common, the daily cost of such a drug habit forced him to start dealing. At first the deals were covert and only between his closest acquaintances, but soon he was dealing with all and sundry. His addiction caused him to be reckless. It was not long before he came to the attention of the police and was caught with two half balls of heroin, a total of 28 grams, commonly known as an ounce. It had cost him $3,000 and after keeping one half ball for himself, he intended to sell the other half ball for $4,000. That way, he hoped to affordably sustain his addiction.

But this way of life was impossible to sustain and it came to an end for Nick at the moment of his arrest. The heroin was in his jeans pocket and he made full admissions to the police that he was intending to sell it. The instructions and facts that he presented to me, as his lawyer, left little to the imagination and a plea of guilty was inevitable. As counsel, I have told many clients that the facts of the allegations and instructions are the only materials I have to work with. Like Michelangelo's marble sculptures, I need solid facts and not soft clay suppositions to create a presentable defence. I sometimes reinforced this edict by saying that I am not a miracle maker and cannot conjure a persuasive defence when there is none. I can only work within the confines of fact and inference. Nick needed a miracle, and for him a miracle was not forthcoming.

He pleaded guilty expediently, by way of a "fast track", and received the maximum discount of 25% for saving the director of public prosecutions the time and money of staging a trial. He received a further discount for the mitigation of not having committed any prior criminal offence and for his profound remorse. He blamed his offending upon his hopeless drug addiction, which was exacerbated by the post-traumatic stress disorder he developed in Vietnam.

Some would argue that Nick should not have been incarcerated but instead should have been provided with specialist mental health care. Some would further argue that drugs should be legalised so that Nick, self-medicating for his trauma, would have been no more than a legitimate customer. Irrespective of anyone's opinions on the matter, however, Nick received a term of two years imprisonment. Once incarcerated, his rehabilitation consisted of going cold turkey and he endured a painful, cringing withdrawal. It would be an understatement to say that his parents were devastated by the downfall and jailing of their only son. He had just turned twenty-three years of age.

All could have ended well with Nick's subsequent rehabilitation and early parole release into society, but for the fact that when he was transferred to a minimum-security prison farm, in preparation of his early release, he was killed while operating the prison tractor. His death was declared a misadventure. His parents continued to grieve for him and remembered a life that was scarred by fighting for the freedom of others. And these injuries in turn, had culminated in their son's tragic death in custody.

# (Attempted) Armed Robbery

Nicole had just turned eighteen and was a pretty, blonde girl with tattoos on her hands and neck. She was softly spoken and generally seemed to have a sweet temperament, but a few bad choices had altered the course of her life. She was now standing in the prisoner's dock in the Supreme Court of Western Australia, an old building built back in 1903.

She was young, and a breath of fresh air in the archaic courtroom, which was adorned with wooden bannisters and leather seats. Obviously, these seats were for the judges and barristers – the accused sat on a wooden bench with barely enough room for the guards to sit on each side of her like bookends. The courtroom looked every year of its age. Even the judge in all his finery looked aged – like an old owl perched high on his podium looking down on his prey. On this occasion, his prey was this young woman who had pleaded guilty to armed robbery. I was her counsel and was entrusted with representing her best interests.

Nicole admitted to using a folding pocketknife to demand money from an unsuspecting fast-food van operator. The van was parked at a poorly lit beachside carpark south of Cottesloe on a humid summer's night. She had been put up to it by her boyfriend, who was barely nineteen years of age himself. That night they were both high on meth, and it was the boyfriend's bright idea that she, his loving girlfriend, should take his pocketknife and rob the van operator. The boyfriend wanted her to do this so they could buy more drugs. Fast food was not on the menu; they were solely fixated on their next hit. The boyfriend had a prior criminal record for this sort of crime and so enlisted his loved one to the task. She was happy to accede to his wishes and obliged him as a show of her devotion and love.

The Court heard in the admitted facts of the crime that they both waited until there were no customers at the van. Nicole then tentatively approached the van to commit the robbery. Unfortunately for her, the van stood high off the ground and her diminutive figure, even holding a knife, did not pose an immediate threat to the man inside. As she approached the van she screamed, "Hey cunt, give me your money or I'll use this," and held out the knife at the full stretch of her arm, still some distance from the van operator's face. Maybe her boyfriend should have given more thought to this plan, but a druggie lives for the present and in the present. Anyway, he got his stooge to commit the robbery as he cowardly looked on from a shadowy distance.

The van operator was surprised by the audacity of this young lady standing below him and holding a knife so small that he could barely see it. His immediate response, spoken like a well-rehearsed drill, was, "Get fucked," and he stepped back further into the safety of the van. She stood there like a shag on a rock with nothing further to say and no money to show for her efforts. The van operator got a good look at her, and was easily able to describe her to police, when they responded to his 000 call. It was fortunate for him and most unfortunate for her that a police car was patrolling nearby, and was on the scene within minutes. The police apprehended her and also extracted and handcuffed the mastermind boyfriend who was found in the shadows nearby. It all happened so quickly that she had barely turned to slink away from the van when the police were upon her. They handcuffed her and took the pathetic knife as an exhibit of the weapon used in the armed robbery, the serious crime with which she was charged.

Having been caught red-handed, Nicole had little option but to plead guilty to the crime. She confessed to the police and told them everything. Consequently, her boyfriend was also charged and after he gave the police a full statement of admissions and pleaded guilty, he received a term of four years imprisonment. These facts were revealed to the judge at Nicole's sentencing, as she stood there facing the music in the Supreme Court. The prosecutor, with some relish, recited the facts of the case to the judge. It was my duty to speak on her behalf and attempt to minimise the inevitable penalty.

She was no longer an accused because she had pleaded guilty to the crime; she was now a prisoner awaiting sentence. An "accused" is a person the police have charged with an offence or crime after being a suspect in the first place. Once an accused has been found guilty, either by their choice of plea or upon conviction after trial, they become an "offender" or "prisoner". Such a person has foregone or lost their presumption of innocence and must face up to punishment – their sentencing. Obviously, the more serious the crime is, the more severe the penalty. Armed robbery is considered to be a very serious offence and can attract a maximum penalty of life imprisonment. It was my duty as her counsel to present to the judge a plea in mitigation.

The challenge for me was to advise the Court of the factors in the case that would encourage a disposition of leniency with respect to my client. Mitigating factors are those matters that are seen to decrease the culpability of the offender or lessen the extent to which the offender should be punished. Further, sentencing statutes and legal precedents regulate the extent to which the judge may reduce a sentence. For example, a plea of guilty may warrant the judge to impose a sentence that is reduced by, say, 25% from the sentence that would have been imposed upon conviction after trial.

In criminal law, the plea in mitigation is extremely important in the sentencing process. It allows the sentencing judge to properly assess the client's level of criminality and to consider the offender's personal antecedents before sentencing that person. These relate to the offender's family background, character, physical and mental well-being, and include education, employment and so on. A plea of guilty demonstrates a willingness by the offender to facilitate the administration of justice and to accept responsibility, and is considered a display of insight and remorse. The level of criminality, a person's perceived involvement in a crime, exists on a continuum of low/minimal to high/severe – for example, from merely aiding and abetting, to being the principal offender. An offender's remorse for what they have done is also an important mitigating factor. If remorse is genuine and not simply regret for being caught, the court can exercise leniency. In such a case, the repentant offender tells the court that he or she has learnt their lesson and will not reoffend.

Nicole was escorted into the courtroom from the bowels of the holding cells. I began my plea in mitigation by agreeing to the material facts as presented by the prosecutor, and then proceeded to try to disassociate my client from her now ex-boyfriend, who had been sentenced with four years immediate imprisonment. I tried to steer the judge away from considering a sentence of parity with the boyfriend's term of imprisonment to one of a non-custodial sanction. The principle of parity states that the co-accused should receive the same sentence for the same offence. I emphasised her youth and naivety and her lovesick vulnerability to her boyfriend, who had put her up to the crime. It was his idea and she was merely his puppet. I highlighted the fact that she had not been in jail before and asked the Court to take pity on her for that fact alone. But before I could finish my sentence, she called out from the dock, "Yes I have."

The judge lifted his head in disbelief. I stood there startled thinking, *I've got the wrong client – I've brought the wrong file to Court.* I felt sure she hadn't been to jail before and wanted to make that crucial point. Her job during sentencing was to keep quiet and let me weave my magic, but she had corrected me – contradicted me – with the words "yes I have." The judge's face grimaced with annoyance, and he glared at me. His expression inferred disgust for my apparent attempt to mislead the Court. I stood there anxiously, having the dual responsibility of being not only her counsel, but also an officer of the Court.

I desperately rummaged through my notes looking for her supposed criminal record, and wondering to myself when and why she had been imprisoned. How could I have overlooked that crucial fact? Shame on me for publicly and formally misleading the Court on such an important point, even if mistakenly. As her thin, screechy voice resonated throughout the courtroom with the words "yes I have," His Honour regained his composure sufficiently to ask, "And when was that? When were you last in jail?" She chirped back, "That was last year, when I visited a friend."

As I heard her response to the judge, I realised I had an idiot for a client, and stopped searching through my file. His Honour looked upon me with some sympathy and said, "It always pays to ask that extra question, doesn't it?" I responded with relief and replied, "Your Honour, she shouldn't be imprisoned just on the stupidity of that comment alone." His Honour grinned and taking a deep breath, sanctioned her to a lenient non-custodial order. I realised there and then the huge discrepancy in intelligence between us all.

Another incident that highlights this discrepancy was when Ian, a long-standing client of mine, shot himself in the leg and had to drive himself to the emergency department of Royal Perth Hospital. What actually happened was that Ian was getting ready to commit an armed robbery on a bank. He had got his stolen sawn-off shotgun and loaded it with two 12-gauge cartridges in readiness for action. He then got his balaclava, gloves and a large bag for all the money, wrote out a mud map and the address of the bank so he wouldn't get lost and put all of these things into the boot of his car. He would do this robbery on his own so that he had full control, and nothing would go wrong.

Ian had committed armed robberies before with other guys but something always went wrong or someone said something that got them caught. So this time he would eliminate those risks by acting alone. He gave a lot of thought to this plan and was confident that he could pull it off. He wore tracksuit pants to help conceal the shotgun and sneakers so he could run away fast. But in all the excitement, he foolishly nestled the shotgun inside his tracksuit against his right leg and as he was stepping into his car, he accidentally blew his calf muscle off the bone with 12-gauge buckshot.

Though in shock and feeling great pain he had sufficient awareness to struggle over to the rear of the car and throw the shotgun into the boot. Abandoning his original plan and now panic-stricken, he drove himself to hospital. The pain was excruciating and his tracksuit looked worse for wear. Not being able to properly use his right foot on the accelerator pedal, he drove rather erratically, though after a twenty-minute ordeal he finally reached the hospital. He stopped haphazardly at the ambulance entrance and left the motor running as he cried for help and a wheel-chair. He quickly got that help and was wheeled off to the emergency theatre. It didn't take long for the medical staff to recognise the injury as a firearm wound and so, as protocol requires, the police were alerted and advised. It didn't take the police long to get to the hospital and search his abandoned car. While still at hospital, Ian was charged with attempted armed robbery and had no choice but to plead guilty as he really didn't have a leg to stand on.

When I received his initial instructions, I was amused by this comedy of events. Fortunately for me, Ian also saw the funny side, now that his injury was on the mend and the comical situation became more apparent. He pleaded guilty some time later and the judge at sentencing concurred with my submission that "Ian was a fool who was far more dangerous to himself than society." His Honour had to give him a severe jail sentence of five years imprisonment without eligibility for parole because he had four prior armed robbery convictions, though this "attempted armed robbery" was nothing more than a blast from the past.

# Man vs Car

I recall representing one particular young man called Scott, who was in his late twenties and charged with a string of offences including dangerous driving causing grievous bodily harm. The allegations were that he had been drinking heavily at a party in Broome, Western Australia, when a fight broke out between his friend and other guests. As Scott went to break up the fight – which had nothing to do with him – he got punched in the face by a brute of a guy. Scott did not retaliate, but in the mayhem, his friend also got bashed. Not wanting any further part of this, Scott retreated, taking his injured friend to his car so they could escape and return to the refuge of their own home. Scott was very drunk and shouldn't have driven, but he did, because he thought it was urgent to get away from the violent scene at the party.

As Scott started driving away, the guy who had punched him came running outside towards him and the car. Scott panicked and accelerated forward, driving straight into the guy and striking him squarely with the grill of the car. The guy glided over the bonnet and smashed into the windscreen with his head and elbow, in what appeared to be slow motion. Scott braked heavily causing the fellow to slide forward and fall off the car and onto the road with an audible thud.

Scott quickly got out of the car, as did his friend. They approached the unconscious man who was lying in the glare of the car headlights. Scott's friend started abusing and swearing at the unresponsive man for damaging the car, calling him a cunt and saying, "Let's make him pay. Scott also took umbrage at the fact that this guy had damaged his windscreen. He was standing over the sprawled guy, and reached down and rifled through his pockets, taking out his wallet. They quickly got back into the car and Scott drove off around the motionless victim. His friend searched through the wallet and found $110, which he decided would go towards compensation for the damage.

The noise of the impact alerted some of the partygoers who came outside to the aid of the victim. Subsequently, witnesses gave police the necessary information that allowed them to lay charges, the most serious of which was dangerous driving causing grievous bodily harm. The allegation specifically charged Scott with using his car with the intent to cause the victim grievous bodily harm. This meant bodily injury of such a nature as to endanger or be likely to endanger life by causing permanent injury to health. The victim's ruptured spleen, broken ribs and fractured head fell within this definition.

During the trial, I represented Scott and raised the defence of emergency. I argued that Scott believed the urgent circumstances to be such that his driving was a reasonable and a necessary response to the sudden threat he and his passenger faced from the attack. This defence was rejected by the jury and did not achieve the acquittal that my client hoped for. It is, however, noteworthy that during his remand period of 10 months in custody awaiting trial, Scott turned to religion and found God. Unfortunately for Scott, though, God couldn't help him with his defence or verdict.

Of course, it is not only when they get caught up in criminal law that a person who has stuffed up turns to religion and finds God. During my short time practising in family law, I was astounded by how a person could ruin their marriage, wreck their family and seriously disrupt their kid's lives, and yet still manage to turn to religion and find God. Faith and hope obviously have something going for them when you're down and out and desperate.

As Scott and his friend found, the motor vehicle can indeed be a weapon, and travelling at high speed is often dangerous – particularly when passing through road intersections. There was a gruesome incident where my client, who was charged with dangerous driving causing death, had driven his Ford utility vehicle through an intersection without giving way to his right, as is required by law. His ute was a crew cab vehicle with an open tray at the back. He later explained that he didn't see the motorbike approaching from his right. The motorbike rider was speeding excessively but did have the right of way at the intersection. Without warning, and still at high speed, the motorbike collided into the rear right side of the utility, causing the bike with its rider to flip and lodge inside the tray.

Police attending the accident could see that the body was headless, as the steel side of the tray had decapitated the rider upon impact. They couldn't find the head of the rider within the close vicinity of the utility and so they extended the search to the surrounding area. Soon, an officer emerged from the scrub at a distance of some 50 metres and approached the scene holding the helmet with the head still inside.

Horrific, gruesome incidents such as these may make the reader feel squeamish and nauseous. However, they highlight the unenviable challenges that police and first responders face on a daily basis as they perform their duties. We owe them a debt of gratitude for their dedication and commitment at the front line of crime and misadventure.

# A Stab in the Dark

Judd was so ugly that his looks challenged even his mother's love for him. Some say that he had a head like a half-eaten pastie. His nose protruded from his square face, which in turn held a mosaic of oddly shaped features. Even in his cubist period, Picasso would have been hard pressed to do better. This ugliness came with a hot temper and an angry attitude.

Judd had previously worked on and off as a labourer in the gold-mining town of Kalgoorlie, Western Australia. His jobs weren't memorable nor did they provide him with any luxury, save for the boozy days he had at the Palace Hotel on the main street of town. When he was out of work, which was often, he would drink from midday until closing time. Fortunately, his rental house was close to the centre of town, which allowed him to walk everywhere. He had permanently lost his driver's licence years before when he was still in his twenties.

Now he was a lot older but not a lot wiser. He was a drunkard and he relied on a government pension to sustain his habitual drinking. Most nights saw him sitting on his usual stool at the Palace main bar, listening to other patrons' raillery, gossip and banter. He would rarely speak, as he was extremely self-conscious of his unappealing looks and the stutter he'd had since childhood. He had been told by welfare workers that he was effectively an orphan, after his single mother became a missing person. He often wondered, while gazing into his beer, what happened to her and if she had left him because he was so hideous.

Because of this, he mainly kept to himself, and consequently was utterly devoid of female company. The nearest he got to a woman, was the odd grope of a skimpy barmaid or an inappropriate comment to a passing female, after he'd had many drinks. Judd's courage and boldness increased with the number of beers he drank and towards the end of the night he would gawk at tipsy females. Sometimes even a smile would break across his cubist face.

One night his smile fell on a woman as drunk as he was, who had also come to the Palace alone. After she had consumed half a dozen Jim Beam and colas he started to look okay to her. She came over with an empty glass, introduced herself and asked him to buy her a drink. He couldn't believe his luck. He didn't care what she looked like, all he cared about was getting her a drink without stuttering and getting her to his place for sex.

His moves were unscripted and spontaneous. He bought a few drinks including the last drink just before closing time. During this drinking session they said little to one another, as the priority was to consume as much liquor as possible before the Palace closed. It was about midnight when they stumbled out of the Palace arm in arm. Nothing was said as Judd escorted her to his place. It wasn't far and before long she was propped up against the front door jamb as he clumsily opened the door. She stumbled inside, took three steps and fell prostrate on the cheap lounge. He did not need an invitation and went straight for her. This was his opportunity to gratify himself, and she lay stupefied like stunned prey in his snare. He took off her shoes, jeans and underpants with less trouble than he had with her top and bra, but eventually he managed to get her naked. The excitement of the moment gave him an adrenaline rush he hadn't experienced in a long time. His rapid movements were incongruous with his befuddled state.

He hadn't had a woman in his house before, let alone a naked one. His house was small. The front door led straight into the lounge room, a cramped room not more than a few paces away from the kitchen, which was divided by an island bench on which sat various utensils, including a large stainless-steel kitchen knife. The knife was styled in one piece of steel with a 12cm embossed handle and a 20cm blade. The blade was sharp, as it hadn't been used much due to his lack of culinary interest.

After taking off his pants, he stood over her preparing to mount her when she suddenly stirred and opened her eyes. At first, she wasn't clear what was happening, but she quickly realised she didn't want to stay and had to get away from him. For his part, Judd was set on having sex with her and was not prepared to let his prey flee. He tried wrestling her back onto the lounge, but she desperately slithered from his grasp and lunged for the front door, which was closed, but fortunately for her, not locked. As she went for the door, he went for the knife, which was not far from his reach. He grabbed the knife and ran at her as she was opening the door. In frustration, he plunged the knife into her, embedding half of the blade into her back at a 45-degree angle. In her panic, she made it outside and onto the next-door neighbour's porch, where she banged on the front door screaming for her life.

Even though it was late at night, the neighbours, an old Italian lady and her daughter, were still watching television when the bedlam started. The old lady, hearing a female voice in distress, rushed to the front door and opened it to see a distraught naked woman standing in front of her. She quickly took off her dressing gown to cover the victim's nakedness, but as she tried to dress her with her gown, she couldn't manage to pull the gown around the back of the victim. She tried a couple of times, unsuccessfully, before she looked behind her, only to see the knife protruding, obstructing her best efforts. The old lady's daughter immediately called the police and an ambulance, and the knife was prudently left in place until she was taken to the hospital. It so happened that despite its deep penetration, the knife miraculously missed vital organs.

During Judd's trial, the jury were mesmerised by the medical photographs and X-rays that showed the knife firmly imbedded in the woman's back. Fortunately for her, she had fully convalesced and was now able to give evidence and refer to her gruesome photos at the Supreme Court trial.

He was charged with attempted murder and I was his counsel at trial. I raised the defence of automatism, submitting to the jury that my client was so drunk, he had stabbed the victim involuntarily. That is, he had behaved automatically, like a machine fuelled by alcohol and acting out a concealed motive of lust. Unfortunately for Judd, I was unsuccessful with that defence. The jury rejected the automaton proposition and unanimously convicted him. After the trial, I had a cold beer at the Palace Hotel and reflected on the legal and factual aspects of our unsuccessful defence. I surmised that maybe that defence had been an unrealistic stab in the dark that was subjugated by the real stab in the dark.

# A Career of Crime

His name was Ben, but he was also known to the authorities by many other aliases, and various combinations of names and dates of birth. His rap sheet that bore these various names had no fewer than 18 pages of crimes and misdemeanours with ten convictions per page. With at least 180 convictions on his criminal record you wouldn't dare call him by any other name than the one he was using at the time. I found out that his nickname was "Torch" which ignited my imagination, though I never dared to ask him for an explanation. He wasn't that bright.

He was a career criminal and told me that he was always resolved to do jail time. For him it was a necessary imposition – as much as paying income tax was for me. Neither of us liked doing it, but such is life. His pragmatism was forthright and blunt. His convictions were mainly of a violent nature, and included assaults and attempted murder. His forte was as a stand-over-man. He weighed 125kg, was over six feet tall, and sported a long rat's tail and smudged DIY prison tattoos. He was strong and fit from his workouts at the prison gym and from all the fights he'd had in the main cellblock. He would fight anyone, anywhere, anytime.

He told me that he didn't mind going to jail as it gave him three regular meals and the opportunity to reacquaint with his associates. It also allowed him time to catch up with the latest gossip from within the criminal world, or the "underground", as he referred to it. He didn't have to pay for a gym membership and always got picked for the football team. The only thing that bothered him about jail, apart from the guards that gave him the shits, was doing time in solitary confinement, that is, in the "special housing unit", also known as the SHU. Because of his violent nature, he often got into fights, which landed him there. Otherwise, his time was occupied by creating makeshift knives. He made these from steel, plastic and anything else that was hard or sharp. Such weapons were used in fighting or for dishing up revenge and settling scores.

On one occasion, Ben was ambushed outside his cell by a large Maori prisoner who used the lid of a baked beans tin to slash his neck. The sharp lid was partly wrapped with cloth where the offender held it and the other end was used as a blade against Ben's skin. The improvised weapon was effective, and left a deep laceration in Ben's neck that fortunately was not fatal but certainly left him bleeding profusely. Instead of calling for the guards, as one would expect, Ben ardently set upon his attacker. Disregarding his own injury, he grabbed his assailant's face with one hand, pulled at the skin of the right cheek and used the fingers of his other hand to gouge the left eye. He later told me that he was most surprised how far he was able to pull and stretch the skin of the face without it ripping. The eye, however, popped out easily.

The assailant came off the worse of the two and ended up losing his eye. He was lucky to not have lost his life as others intervened and broke up the fight. After receiving eight stitches to the neck wound, Ben wore the scar with pride. Unfortunately for the assailant, his time in hospital was considerable as the surgeons tried to reattach his eyeball and save the eye, without success.

Unsurprisingly, no complaint was made by either inmate and both were spared time in solitary confinement, which is the most severe sanction imposed by prison authorities on recalcitrant inmates. It is a small cell with no natural light and only the bare necessities of a bed, toilet and sink. Being confined to the SHU allows the inmate a daily outing of no more than two hours in the exercise yard located outside the confinement cell. Their time is otherwise spent inside the dingy cell for days and sometimes weeks on end. The punishment doesn't teach the inmate anything. It only removes him from the mainstream of prison life for the convenience of management.

At the time that this occurred, Ben was on remand

awaiting my advice about an incident for which he was charged with kidnapping. As with all things Ben was involved in, this was no run-of-the-mill kidnapping, it was against a questionable male, and the story had an interesting twist.

Ben was owed $1,500 by his "friend", who repeatedly stalled the repayment. That could well have been because Ben was in jail most of the time and was unable to personally call up the loan. Anyway, some months passed and Ben was released on parole. He wanted his money, which he now desperately needed to rebuild his life and go straight, as he had promised the parole board. The scenario of Ben's life was a revolving door of jail and short stints of freedom before more jail. The debtor must have been counting on that fact, and was hoping "Torch" would be back inside too soon to call in his debt. However, Ben was committed to his rehabilitation this time, and was very motivated on this occasion to have his loan repaid, as he needed the cash to stay on the straight and narrow.

After asking his friend nicely for the $1,500, which endeavour came to no avail, he took the unsurprising measure of extracting and collecting the debt personally the very next day. As words had already failed, this time he would approach the debtor with a persuasive baseball bat. In broad daylight, Ben approached the verandah of the front door of the debtor's house with baseball bat in hand. There was no need for a disguise as he figured he was well within his rights to reclaim his money.

The debtor opened the door and was met with a blow from the bat. Ben bashed it onto the skull of the debtor, who lunged at him, causing Ben to step back and volley another blow to the skull, this time breaking the bat. Ben abandoned the broken end and instead grabbed the debtor by the hair and dragged him inside the house. The debtor was semi-conscious and only just able to respond to Ben's demands, telling him where he could find his wallet. Ben helped himself to the cash from the wallet, only $230, but a promising start to a repayment scheme. He was confident that he would now get the balance in a timely manner. As he was leaving, Ben announced to the debtor who was lying on the floor, bleeding and looking bewildered, that he would be back the following week for the balance, and demanded that the debtor not breathe a word of this to the police. The debtor shook his bloodied head most cooperatively. Ben was now assured that the debtor who was also his supposed friend, would not dare go to the police or cause any trouble.

Sure enough, Ben came around the following week at the same time, this time without a baseball bat as he felt sure the debtor had got his message loud and clear. The debtor answered the door more circumspectly, this time, opening it only as far as the new security latch allowed. He wore a bandage on his head and peered at Ben through the gap. It was most pleasing to Ben that without any further demand, he saw the balance of the debt in folded cash being gingerly pushed through the gap towards him. Ben stuck his right boot inside the door gap preventing it from closing as he counted out the cash that totalled exactly the balance of $1,270. He blurted again that the police were to be kept out of it and heard the debtor submissively reply, "No problem. I'm not going to the police. We're square now."

Ben felt reassured that the police would not be involved as a few months had gone by without any problem and the debt had been settled and squared off. The debtor was true to his word and in accordance with the moral code between criminals, he made no complaint to the police and went about his business with something of a sore head.

At the time of this incident, however, and occurring in parallel to it, the debtor's business was dealing in drugs. Unbeknown to Ben, the debtor was a person of interest to the police and was under constant surveillance as a suspect in an extensive drug ring. Some five months later, Ben was shocked to find two policemen at the door, who subsequently arrested him for deprivation of liberty and serious assault. Ben, who again became my client, was flabbergasted. He knew the debtor would not and did not blab to the police, so he was perplexed as to why he was being charged for these matters without a complaint having been made. In his mind, they belonged to ancient history,

This is exactly what he asked the police. They told him that they had a surveillance camera pointed at the debtor's front door, as he was a suspect in a major drug investigation. Further, they told Ben that they had now completed their investigations and had arrested the drug dealers they were monitoring, and now wanted to talk to my client about the excellent high-definition footage of him visiting the house with a baseball bat, and breaking it over the head of their suspect.

The evidence against Ben was overwhelming and so he reluctantly pleaded guilty at the first opportunity. By his expedited plea, Ben saved the state and the director of public prosecutions time and money, which enabled the sentencing court to show its statutory appreciation by granting Ben a 25% reduction on the sentence that he would and should have received. He still got a total of four years straight imprisonment without any eligibility for parole, due to his extensive criminal history. As fate would have it, his "friend" and former debtor was now a convicted drug dealer and had been sentenced according-ly, also receiving four years jail. Fortunately for him, he was kept in a separate cell wing to my client.

# Between the Devil and the Deep Blue Sea

The high seas can maketh the man. The ominous depth of the ocean and its incessant waves have the power to sculpt a character from a tender young sailor to a rugged tugboat captain. Lyle was such a person. He went to sea as a youngster and through diligent studies at night school, learnt the theory and later accomplished the skills needed to command and steer a ship. However, as with many forthright men, he harboured a flaw. On the one hand he was intelligent and competent, but on the other hand he was a bogan: coarse, insensitive and pretty rough around the edges. He was an alpha male who had no qualms bossing his crew around and calling the shots as the captain.

After many years at sea he landed the coveted job of being a captain on a tugboat in the Pilbara region of northern Western Australia. He was forty-two years old and unsurprisingly single, probably because of his personality – or rather, the lack of it – and his inability to settle in one place. He blamed his job for not having a family, but his acquaintances had no doubt that it was his dominant and bullish attitude that made him a loner.

During the prosperous mining boom in the early years of the new millennium, Lyle's employers paid him $300,000 per annum for his competency and captaincy. His duties as a tugboat captain included ushering the iron ore super tankers in and out of port as they made their long journey to and from China. On these occasions, he had the responsibility of positioning these ships safely into their designated berths. There were no set work rosters and he had to be available at any time for when the ships approached the port. The long hours of work sometimes became tedious, especially when the seas were calm and circumstances uneventful.

After a few months of constant work, he obtained some leave that was sufficient to allow him a short holiday in Perth. He went alone. During this holiday, he had been invited to a 40th birthday party in Fremantle. The birthday party included a mixed bunch of people from the surrounding suburbs and was hosted in a quaint terrace house.

It was a raucous party with loud music and about fifty

revellers who were all having a good time. The alcohol flowed freely, and some illicit drugs were being handed around. Lyle hadn't binged on alcohol for a few months. He was now drinking quickly and was having a great time. It didn't take long for him to get tipsy and by the time it approached midnight, he'd had a skin full of alcohol and was very drunk. As if that wasn't enough, he had also smoked some ice with an acquaintance in the laneway to the back of the house. He had never before experienced such a concoction. The combination of booze and drugs stirred the bogan within Lyle. All of a sudden he was back at the party aggressively arguing with a stranger about something that he later couldn't remember and which couldn't have been important.

During the argument, they started pushing each other. Lyle was only about 165cm tall and had a medium to slight build, whereas the other guy, who was younger, stood 190cm tall and had a bulky frame. The pushing quickly progressed to wrestling. Onlookers started to move away rather than intervene in the fight. Chairs went everywhere as Lyle desperately grappled with the stronger combatant. Lyle's shirt was ripped and he could feel wetness on his back, which he hoped was beer.

The combatant had Lyle pinned against the wall and started gouging at his left eye. Lyle screamed for him to let go of his eye, however, the young fellow not only had a firm grip of Lyle's face but also was forcing his right index finger deep into Lyle's left eye. The pain was excruciating and Lyle's vision became blurred. He was still holding onto his assailant with both hands but wasn't causing him anything like the pain he himself was suffering. As the combatant applied more pressure on the eye, he moved his right thumb around Lyle's nose and into his mouth, seeking better purchase against Lyle's teeth so he could gouge deeper into the eye. With the combatant's thumb now in his mouth, Lyle fought back in the only way he could – by biting the thumb.

He bit so hard that his teeth went right through the thumb and bit it off at the first joint. Lyle's mouth was filled with blood and the combatant quickly let go of Lyle's face and withdrew his finger from the eye. As they released their grip on each other, Lyle found the piece of thumb in his mouth, and reactively spat it out where it landed on the floor near the family dog. The obese red heeler, who had been moping under the table during the party, jumped at the thumb in a flash and swallowed it in one gulp. The chance of grafting the thumb tip back on the remaining digit disappeared down the throat of the family dog.

The crowd of revellers became quickly subdued and were trying to work out what had just happened. The screaming and obscenities that came from the now victim's mouth indicated that he was suffering from a serious injury, and his bleeding hand and Lyle's bloodied mouth reinforced the concerns of the onlookers. When the ambulance arrived, the victim was taken, thumb-less, to hospital. Soon after, the police arrested Lyle, who later became my client. He was charged with assault occasioning grievous bodily harm, with the allegation that he caused permanent injury to the victim. In other words, it was alleged that he used excessive force that was not justified in the circumstances. Lyle's explanation was that as a result of the fight and his eye being gauged, he took the reasonable and necessary step to disarm (or in this case, to dis-thumb) the combatant by biting his thumb, which he had conveniently found in his mouth.

The matter went to trial before a judge and jury. Lyle had an excellent employment record and no criminal history. He presented as a very credible defendant and had every chance of getting off the serious charge. The only problem for him was that he had bitten right through the thumb joint, severing it in two, and the top was still missing. The looming question for the jury was whether his action was reasonable and justified in the context of the fight. After some considerable deliberation, the jury returned a verdict of guilty, meaning that the severance of the thumb was deemed unreasonable and excessive, and so, unjustified.

At sentencing, I presented to the Court Lyle's excellent personal antecedence and labelled Lyle's criminal act (which upon the jury's verdict, it was now classified as) as an aberration of his character. Further, I argued that he had learnt his lesson not to mix booze and drugs and was unlikely to reoffend. It was also mitigating that he had lost his highly paid job at a difficult age for re-employment and would suffer disdain from his colleagues. While jail was not a place for this man of the sea, that was exactly where he was forced to berth after receiving a four-year sentence.

The sentence seemed inordinate and so an appeal against it was lodged in the Court of Criminal Appeal. The ground of appeal was that the sentence, when considered in all the circumstances of the case, was manifestly excessive. The submissions attempted to lure the Appeal Court judges to reduce the sentence, but unfortunately, they did not bite.

# Getting Away with Murder

Drug dealing can be a dangerous enterprise for many people, including the drug dealer himself. Such danger comes not only from the police but also from other dealers and suppliers. In the town of Kalgoorlie, Western Australia, methamphetamine is as valuable as the gold the town is famous for.

Twenty-four-year-old Blair was a well-liked resident of Kalgoorlie, and a drug user, who had become involved in the insidious business of drug dealing. His friends knew him as a person who lived on the edge and was willing to take any risk and defy any odds. He was very good looking and used to brag that he wanted to live the life-style of a rock star despite having the affliction of poverty. The reality was that he lived by himself in a granny flat behind a humble house in the hot and dusty mining town.

As if that wasn't bad enough, it wasn't long before he accumulated significant drug debts by using more drugs than he sold, and his suppliers demanded payment. The fact of the matter was that the debt was owing and his time to pay it had run out. According to the underworld code and as a co-accused later revealed at trial, he now "had to pay with his life."

On a night in late summer, a group went to Blair's granny flat. As they approached his front door he opened it and welcomed them in. These drug creditors and their associates totalled four in number ranging in age from forty-eight down to twenty-five. My client, Jordan, the youngest, was between mining jobs at the time. He was also a well-liked resident of Kalgoorlie and a meth user, though to a lesser extent. Unbeknownst to Blair, the group had weapons with them, and a large blue canvas bag, about two meters long: large enough to carry a body. The bag had previously been used to transport a bicycle, but it now would be used for carting weapons, and maybe a corpse.

When Blair opened his front door and invited them inside, he apparently did not suspect any trouble, however, the opposite was true. Very soon, he was overpowered by the group who restrained him by cable tying his hands and feet together. The evidence at trial was that whilst "hog tied", Blair was tortured in his own home during which time his right ring finger was crudely amputated. A machete, a knife, two iron bars and a sword were produced and used in the brutal attack. The attackers inflicted severe head injuries to Blair, and stabbed his neck, cutting his jugular vein. The cable ties incapacitated Blair and he was powerless to defend himself. He also sustained injuries to his eyes consistent with a great degree of force having been inflicted upon his eyeballs and around his eye sockets.

The coroner found alcohol, meth and amphetamines in Blair's toxicological analysis, which was possibly the reason he seemed blasé when they arrived at his house. The medical pathologist at trial listed the numerous injuries inflicted upon the deceased and then surmised that the cause of death was either due to blunt-force injuries to the head and neck or a penetrating injury to the neck that cut the veins, causing him to bleed out.

Further evidence was led that Blair's body had been dragged around before it was removed from his home. There was a pool of blood and a dark stain on the floor of the kitchen, and bloody drag marks smeared across the living area. Numerous stains consistent with drips of blood were also found on the kitchen floor and throughout the living area, on the carpet, cushions and items of furniture. There were also a number of shoe prints transferring blood across the kitchen and living room floors. The experts for the prosecution concluded that Blair had been positioned on the kitchen floor, where he bled profusely from his head and neck, causing the pool of blood. They surmised that he was then dragged across the floor and into the living area by at least two people, who had walked over the bloody scene and traipsed blood across the floor.

After the attack, one of the assailants pulled out of the wall and destroyed the CCTV home surveillance equipment Blair had installed. The deceased was then stuffed into the blue canvas bag, taken to the rear of the parked station wagon and placed inside. All four assailants travelled with the body to the home of the oldest of the group, who was the main instigator of this crime.

It just so happened that at the time, this assailant had a prostitute living with him and selling drugs for him. It transpired that she had met him before, as a client, and that they had developed a rapport of mutual needs – as much as a drug dealer could with a prostitute. Thereafter, he let her stay at his house rent free and in exchange she cleaned and shopped for him and more importantly, satisfied his sexual desires and sold his drugs.

When they arrived at the house, the attackers carried Blair's body from the vehicle to the bathroom and placed it into the bathtub. There, they decapitated the body and dismembered it into nine separate parts, being the head, right arm and left arm, right and left thighs, right and left lower legs, torso and the right ring finger. It appears that two knives and a machete were used to perform this gruesome dismemberment. They then dumped the body parts into a blue council wheelie bin and sealed the lid with an adhesive and black gaffer tape.

During this gory process, Jordan was sent to the local shops to buy four bottles of liquid bleach and some draino. Upon his return, he found the prostitute, under sufferance, putting on rubber gloves and beginning to clean the bathroom of the congealed blood, hair, scalp and flesh that was everywhere, particularly in the bathtub drain. She cleaned for a long time, trying to get rid of the evidence, which included small pieces of flesh that she threw into the toilet. After cleaning the bathroom to the best of her ability, she then rinsed her gloves and hung them with pegs on the Hills Hoist clothesline to dry them in the hot desert wind. The gloves were still hanging on the clothesline when police arrived the following day. Similarly, the loaded blue wheelie bin was standing in the adjoining shed. The items told a grizzly tale.

During the clean-up, Jordan and the other young accomplice were ordered to start a fire in the backyard barbeque pit, which they obediently did. All of the offenders then removed their clothing and thongs and threw them into the barbeque fire in order to destroy their apparel, which was blood-stained and incriminating. Despite their best efforts to cover up the crime, the Major Crime Squad and police forensics found abundant evidence including part of Blair's finger that was wedged beneath the bathroom door.

Jordan and the other three co-accused were separately represented by defence lawyers, and each pleaded not guilty. They stood trial together on the charge of murder.

The jury were reminded that even though all four co-accused were being tried together for economic reasons, there were in fact four separate trials being heard simultaneously. The jury were therefore required to consider each case separately and return a verdict for each accused. Jordan's defence was that of duress. He admitted to applying the cable ties and assisting in restraining the victim and disposing of the body, but claimed that he was not criminally responsible for murder, as he was acting under duress. The duress came from the oldest two assailants, who threatened him with his own life if he did not obey and do as he was commanded.

At the conclusion of the seven-week trial, the two older defendants aged forty-eight and thirty-nine years were both convicted by the jury of murder. Fortunately for my client and the twenty-nine-year-old accused, they were both convicted of the lesser crime of manslaughter. At sentencing, I submitted to the Court that Jordan was still a young man at twenty-five years of age, who was suffering low self-esteem and had been easily influenced by the older co-accused. He had been cajoled by the two older individuals who were almost twice his age. One, in fact, was Jordan's previous supervisor on a mine site at which he had worked and been his subordinate. Jordan complained that he had been domineered and was the victim of duress, which the jury, after deliberating for more than two days, accepted, returning a verdict of manslaughter. Further, my client expressed emotions of distress and trauma to the police immediately after the incident, and had cooperated with the investigating authorities by handing himself in. He also candidly nominated the other three co-accused and divulged their involvement and roles.

Whilst in remand custody, Jordan received death threats and was seriously assaulted by other prisoners. He was therefore segregated from the other inmates for his own safety. He had heard on the prison grapevine that there was a contract of $80,000 for his life. During sentencing, I highlighted to the Court that Jordan had an excellent opportunity to be rehabilitated and that upon his release he was likely to lead a law-abiding life. He was a qualified rigger, which put him in good stead for full-time employment upon his release and he had previously worked as a crane operator. Finally, I told the Court that Jordan had barely any criminal convictions and had the full support of his family and friends to assist him with his future. It was also encouraging to note that Jordan had abstained from drugs since the day of his arrest some 18 months before and was motivated to stay clean in the future.

After considering all these submissions and mitigating circumstances, the two oldest assailants who were convicted of murder each received a life sentence with a minimum of 23 years imprisonment to be served before they were eligible for parole. My client and the other offender were each convicted of manslaughter and received eight years imprisonment with eligibility for parole after serving at least six years imprisonment. The sentencing judge in respect to Jordan said that he considered my client's involvement to be that of immature bravado fuelled by the feelings induced by methamphetamine intoxication. Overall, Jordan was relieved by the jury's verdict and pleased with the reasonable sentence.

The victim's mother had travelled to Perth from Queensland for the trial, attended each day of the hearing and was also present for the verdicts. The presiding judge thanked her and the members of her family for their respectful behaviour throughout the trial. His Honour also thanked the jury members for their diligence during the long trial, which had involved a great deal of disturbing and distressing evidence.

During this macabre trial, one of the forensic officers in his evidence made a startling revelation. He said that when the blood at the bottom of the blue rubbish bin was tested forensically for DNA, it revealed that some of it belonged to three other persons in addition to the victim. The investigation is ongoing in relation to the apparent and suspicious demise of those other three people, and so someone, most probably, is still getting away with murder.

# Man's Best Friend

One evening in the winter of 1999, what started out as a routine drug bust took a different twist, and ended up a lot more embarrassing than being found with meth in the closet.

Gus was a forty-two-year-old truck driver. He was married with two children, a daughter aged nine and a son aged six, and they had a family dog – a bull mastiff called Brutus. Gus operated his own business as a contractor in the busy transport industry. He was a family man and mainly kept to himself, except for some drug dealing on the side to supplement his cash reserves.

Over a considerable period of time, he came to the attention of the police conducting drug investigations around the suburbs of Perth in the late 1990s. His truck, bearing his name and logo, had mysteriously appeared in various questionable locations during police surveillance operations. As such, there were sufficient reasons for the police to obtain a Misuse of Drugs Act search warrant for him and his home.

Unaware of the police suspicions, Gus and his family, including Brutus, were watching television one cold winter's evening when, at around 8pm, no fewer than ten police officers arrived unannounced to act upon the warrant. They pounded on the front door demanding entry. The television program was suddenly irrelevant and all the family's attention was on the front door, which Gus opened with some trepidation. The officers streamed into the house and handcuffed Gus on suspicion of drug dealing before reading him his rights as an arrested suspect. They advised the rest of the family that they were not under arrest and were free to leave, or could stay seated in the lounge room whilst the police conducted a full search of the home.

When the police concluded their search, Gus was charged and arrested for being in possession of 32 grams of methamphetamine, 30 clip seal bags and a set of electronic scales. These items were all found in his wardrobe. He was bailed at $10,000 surety and remanded to appear in court the following month.

Unbeknownst to Gus, when the police had arrived, his nine-year-old daughter, who was most confused about the sudden intrusion, asked the nearest officer, "Are you here because Daddy has been playing with the dog's willy?" The officer stopped dead in his tracks and looked down at the young girl, containing his reaction of surprise. He quickly ushered her into a neighbouring room to delve deeper into this rather worrying and crass story. She then explained in great detail to the officer how her father, while watching Today Tonight on TV after their family dinner, would wank Brutus the dog while he lay on his back by the fire, with his paws in the air. She complained to the officer, saying that she'd told her dad it was disgusting wanking "his little red rocket", but that he had fobbed her off, saying, "The dog loves it." The officer wrote down her statement, which she had given, believing the police were there for that sole purpose.

Whilst still at the police station, Gus was shocked and embarrassed when the officer read out the charges, which, though mainly pertaining to the drugs, also included a final charge of "carnal knowledge of an animal" – namely Brutus the bull mastiff. In due course, Gus decided he was not prepared to go against his daughter's story. In any event, it was the truth and he didn't want the matter to be aired in front of a jury of his peers in open court. He would rather "let sleeping dogs lie".

Gus pleaded guilty to the drugs and carnal knowledge charges and came up for sentencing. The sentencing judge first dealt with the drug convictions and ordered a sentence of three years, which reflected the quantity and purity of the drugs. The judge then turned to the last count on the indictment, that being the matter involving Brutus. He chastised Gus for such a lewd act and described it as totally unacceptable and immoral, especially in front of his daughter. Gus retorted from the dock, "I didn't hear Brutus complaining!"

I argued that Gus should receive a concurrent sentence with the drugs convictions, however, I was obviously barking up the wrong tree as the judge disagreed with me and ordered an extra one-year imprisonment for the dog wanking. Despite Gus's wish that the matter not go public, word travels fast on the prison grapevine and it wasn't long before his fellow inmates were aware of his pet hobby and would woof at him every time he came past.

Sometimes it's a dog's life.

# Alvin's Six-Shooter

Hakea Prison is a maximum security and remand correctional institution, which derives its name from the Hakea plant, a striking Western Australian native tree that blossoms in clusters of red and orange flowers known as "red pokers." The beauty of this plant is in direct contrast to the harsh reality of the prison. The prison is the main centre for custodial processing of all remand and sentenced prisoners in the state of Western Australia. It is always overcrowded, primarily due to the increasing prevalence of drugs in the community.

It was in these stark premises, that I met a new client who had been charged with attempted murder. As I checked in at the official visits centre and was allocated my interview office, I was told by the staff that my client was one of the most dangerous prisoners they have had to deal with. There was concern on their faces, which I duly noted. As a matter of security, I was provided with a distress alarm, which I hung around my neck with my visitor's pass. Further, safety procedures also required me to sit near the door of the interview room so that in case of any emergency or attack on my person I could readily escape, or receive the immediate help of guards.

My new client's name was Alvin and he did not stand tall but was a stocky and well-built thirty-eight-year-old. His face was clean cut and he had a schoolboy haircut that belied his bad reputation. He wore standard issue prison greens comprising velcro shoes and an olive-green tracksuit with a round neck jumper, which exposed his tattoos and thick neck. Due to the serious charge he was facing and the staff's build-up of his dangerous persona, I thought I'd open my introduction to him with some levity. As he walked into the room I said, "Alvin, how are you? Interesting name. Is that Alvin as in The Chipmunks?" He glared at me and said, "Not funny, cunt!" It was I who felt like a chipmunk as I hastily swallowed my faux pas. It was not a great start to our first meeting and this important interview.

When I had composed myself, I listened while he told me his side of the story of how he and his girlfriend had been woken at 3am by a supposed friend who wanted to buy a gun and share some drugs. It just so happened that Alvin did have an old .38 special revolver and some ammunition and was happy to sell this "orphan" (the nickname for a stolen or unregistered gun). In fact, he told the friend he wanted $3,000 for it and was only prepared to get out of bed for that amount and to do the deal. The location for the meeting was to be a vacant house known to both men.

When Alvin and his girlfriend got to the place they went inside and met up with the friend and his girlfriend. At the time Alvin's left arm was incapacitated – he called it a "dead arm" – due to having received a "hot shot" of meth from his girlfriend the preceding week. His left hand was cradled in the left pocket of his hoodie jumper to disguise the fact that he was somewhat disabled and therefore vulnerable to attack from predatory gangsters or opportunistic "customers". The house was empty of furniture and there were only some old milk crates to sit on and use as a table. Alvin didn't plan to be there long. It was the middle of the night and he had got out of bed solely to sell the revolver for a handsome profit.

Before the deal was struck, his friend enticed Alvin and both the girlfriends to share some meth. They smoked the drug rather unceremoniously, using an old crack pipe whilst seated on overturned crates in the austere room. Alvin was keen to get on with the transaction and produced the revolver, which for some unknown reason, he had loaded. The revolver bore six bullets in its revolving magazine. He put it on the crate between them and asked for the cash. The friend produced it, and Alvin started to count it with his good hand. Whether it was the effect of the drugs or mischief he had calculated earlier, the friend did not intend to pay anything for the stolen revolver. He had brought a large Bowie hunting knife with him. Alvin didn't know that, however, and didn't know what to make of his friend's attitude. He simply wanted cash for the revolver and recompense for the inconvenience of being dragged out of bed in the middle of the night.

Apparently noticing Alvin's incapacity, the so-called friend, without warning, produced the large knife and lunged at Alvin, gutting him through the abdomen. The wound was significant enough to cause his intestines to slop out and unfurl towards the ground. Grabbing the loaded gun, Alvin jumped to his feet and started shooting. However, the friend kept coming at Alvin with the knife, causing him to stumble backwards while he pulled the trigger three more times. Alvin aimed below the friend's waist so as to only stop him and not kill him. Five of the six bullets hit their target in the man's scrotum, belly and legs. Alvin, unable to use his "dead arm," wrapped his intestines around his right forearm while still holding the revolver, and made for the back door. His friend still kept coming, lurching after him for a short distance before collapsing on the floor in agony.

Alvin's girlfriend rushed him to the hospital in his Holden ute, which she had never driven before. She drove fast and erratically to Royal Perth Hospital, and was of course still high on meth. Unfortunately, with the stress of each tight corner, Alvin's intestines exited further, causing him excruciating pain and he abused her at each turn. Just as Alvin was being admitted into the emergency department, his friend also arrived, hobbling into the emergency reception with a bloodied towel wrapped around his waist.

The police were alerted and initiated an investigation during which Alvin was most uncooperative, adhering instead to the underworld code of honour and silence. During the investigation it became apparent that Alvin's supposed friend had himself previously been acquitted of a murder charge in which he had pleaded self-defence when he stabbed a man to death during an altercation at a house party. The striking resemblance of this previous matter to Alvin's current predicament was uncanny.

Alvin was initially charged with attempted murder but this was downgraded to a charge of assault occasioning grievous bodily harm, as Alvin had deliberately aimed below the waist and had no intent to kill. The charge alleged that my client shot his friend without excuse or justification causing him life threatening and/or permanent injury.

As time passed, both men recovered from their serious wounds. Of course, Alvin's defence at trial was one of self-defence. He had a significant scar on his abdomen that corroborated this evidence before the jury. The trial was rather extraordinary when all of the facts were revealed. I recall a male juror wincing at the forensic evidence that illustrated the path the bullet had taken through the man's scrotum, just missing his testicles.

At some of Alvin's interviews with me he re-enacted

the drama. He would jump up from his seat and spring backwards in the interview room like a tiger, resting his "dead" left arm against his chest and pretending to shoot with the other, his index finger protruding like a barrel and his thumb upright like a gun sight. He would then theatrically mime with his shooting hand how he had gathered up and supported his unravelling intestines. It was a sight to behold and his running commentary was second to none.

My client's impressive re-enactment to the jury, together with his declaration on oath that he had shot his attacker below the waist only to stop himself from being stabbed to death, won the day and the jury returned a verdict of not guilty. Obviously, the jury accepted the fact that my client's actions were justified, even though the circumstances were excruciating.

## AUTHORITY FOR PUBLICATION

I also give permission to you's any photo's henry
seds fit to put in his book from my face book
account's *Alvin Kirwan*

I, Alvin Kirwan, inmate of Albany Regional Prison, hereby give my full authority
and consent to Mr Henry Sklarz to use my Christian name "Alvin" in the book
and/or article, which he intends to publish referring to my engagement of his
services as defence counsel in criminal law.

*Alvin Kirwan*

Alvin Kirwan


I would like to thankyou for representing
me and the Not Guilty verdicts henry
I look forward to reading your
Book an if it ends up a bestseller
surly I can get a free trial with
your represtation Halla take it
easy
          sincerly
               Alvin Kirwan